DATE DUE

WALT WHITMAN

*A Study
in the Evolution of
Personality*

WALT
WHITMAN

*A Study
in the Evolution of
Personality*

BY

JAN CHRISTIAN SMUTS

Edited, with a Foreword, by
ALAN L. McLEOD
Rider College

WAYNE STATE UNIVERSITY PRESS · *Detroit · 1973*

Published simultaneously in Canada
by the Copp Clark Publishing Company
517 Wellington Street, West
Toronto 2B, Canada.

Library of Congress Cataloging in Publication Data
Smuts, Jan Christian, 1870–1950.
   Walt Whitman: a study in the evolution of personality.
   Includes bibliographical references.
   1. Whitman, Walt, 1819–1892.
PS3231.S6 1972   811'.3   72-4123
ISBN 0-8143-1484-8

"There is something greater (is there not?) than all the science and poems of the world—above all else, like the stars shining eternal—above Shakspere's plays, or Concord Philosophy, or Art of Angelo or Raphael—something that shines elusive, like beams of Hesperus at evening—high above all the vaunted wealth and pride—prov'd by its practical outcropping in life, each case after its own concomitants—the intuitive blending of divine love and faith in a human emotional character—blending for all, the unlearn'd, the common, and the poor."

"Elias Hicks," 717-25.

Contents

Foreword

*

by Alan L. McLeod

JAN CHRISTIAN SMUTS (1870–1950), former prime minister of the Union of South Africa and a field marshal of the British army, stands with Winston Churchill, Woodrow Wilson, and Mohandas Gandhi in the forefront of world statesmen of the first half of this century. Like these others, his friends and colleagues, he was able in an extraordinary degree to combine philosophical position with political policy, and to bring to public life much of the benefit of his reading, speculation, and insight.

And if these others are today better known and understood than Smuts, the eventual publication and study of the Smuts archives is likely to correct the situation. Though Churchill was at the epicenter of world events and led an active life, yet he lacked the academic experience and disposition that Smuts so singularly enjoyed; though Gandhi had a perhaps more substantial and subtle philosophical and contemplative preparation, his life kept him apart from strenuous physical and military experience; though Wilson was steeped in academic, religious, and political experience, he too had little direct contact with the general population through military and similar exploits, and projected an uninspiring, eremitical mien. Smuts, more than any of his contemporaries in world affairs, seems to have been the "whole man."

For fifty years, until his death in 1950, the political life of South Africa bore Smuts's stamp. Though born a British subject in Cape Province, he migrated to the Transvaal and became its attorney general, at age 28, under the legendary Paul Kruger. After finding it impossible to negotiate a satisfactory solution of the Boer-British antipathies in the Transvaal, Smuts deployed his commandos with tactical brilliance and devastating effect. And it was he who, not oblivious of the deleterious effects of the Boer War, nonetheless led South Africa to Union and self-government, to military victory in German South-West Africa, to membership in the League of Nations and the Commonwealth of Nations—organizations which were products of his prescience.

For fifty years—from his participation in the Boer War and its settlement—Smuts was a major figure in world affairs. He gave valuable counsel to Lord Allenby in planning the Palestine Campaign of World War I; contributed meaningfully to the deliberations of the Imperial War Cabinet; proposed, in a speech on 15 December 1918, the establishment of a League of Nations, and saw this and its successor, the United Nations, become instruments—though imperfect ones—for the maintenance of world peace.

Sir Robert Menzies, former Australian prime minister, commenced his Smuts Memorial Lecture at Cambridge in 1960 with a succinct appreciation of his former imperial colleague:

Jan Christian Smuts was one of the most remarkable men in modern history. He was a scholar in the finest sense; a soldier of remarkable distinction; a South African statesman who made an imperishable contribution to the history and institutions of his own land; a Commonwealth statesman whose towering abilities made him a commanding figure, the trusted confidant and adviser of the giant of the age, Winston Churchill; a world leader, "the very wind of whose name"—if I may borrow that great phrase spoken by J. M. Barrie about the Scots—"has swept to the ultimate seas." [1]

Throughout his lifetime Smuts was a serious student of philosophy—especially of German philosophy—having studied it at Stellenbosch, Strasbourg, and Cambridge; and when he was leading his commando forces in the Boer War he carried in his saddlebag two books: a Greek New Testament and Kant's *Critique of Pure Reason*.

In a sense, these two books represented the two traditions—those of religious belief and intellectual inquiry—to which Smuts was exposed in his formative years and that he endeavored to harmonize throughout his life, both in his everyday political activities and in his lasting philosophical speculations. The New Testament was the unquestioned source of divine authority for his Dutch Calvinist family and their countrymen, who took heed of its emphasis upon faith, good works, the righteousness of the elect, and the unimpeachable primacy of the moral law. Kant, on the other hand, presented the attractive concept of an integration of logic and metaphysics, formulated in the transcendental philosophy that was based on reason, experience, and the moral law. When, to Kant's insistence that the only real world is that of thought—which is continuous with external nature—we add Hegel's dialectical method (frequently alluded to with favor by Smuts), we can appreciate Smuts's delight in finding that he was able to postulate a synthesis of these two philosophies and methodologies.

His own philosophy, as it finally developed, propounded that evolution, whether of the individual personality or of social or political entities, was a series of ever more comprehensive integrations of forces and ideas, of positions and policies. The practical application of his philosophy in South Africa was his Union Party, which set for itself the reconciliation of Boer and British interests and their utilization in the commonweal. It was subsequently extended to interracial affairs as he attempted to formulate a policy—albeit of separate development—that would preserve the essential character of Bantu life and institutions without altering traditional European interests and culture. Under less enlightened leadership his policy degenerated into apartheid. In the wider sphere of international affairs, Smuts's philosophy led directly and almost inevitably to support for the League of Nations as a rational means of synthesizing the divergent forces at play between nations; for he envisioned the League as something on a higher level than such predecessor organizations as the Congress system that followed the Napoleonic wars, something more than a regulatory body, something akin to a multinational commonwealth and tribunal. And those aspects of the Treaty of Versailles that imposed harsh reparations he criticized as illogical, punitive, and unjust. On this subject his thinking was later found to be more advanced than most of his contemporaries'. In the transformation of the British Empire into the Commonwealth of Nations as a result of the Statute of Westminster, Smuts saw a further proof of his evolutionist or holist philosophy, and he regarded the new Commonwealth as an exemplary means of assuring the rights of subscribing members while retaining the necessary rights and prerogatives of the initiating power; that is, he saw it as a logical, just, and outstanding growth in international government. With the shortcomings of the League and the Commonwealth revealed, he nonetheless believed that the United Nations would even more surely provide mankind with a form of international government and conciliation that would guarantee comity and progress. In the formation of all three international organizations Smuts took a significant, even a leadership, role; in all three he appears to have seen the fulfilment of his philosophical belief in the continuity of development, in social evolution.

In 1891 Smuts won the Ebden Scholarship to Cambridge. During his sojourn in England, reading first at Cambridge, then in London, for his law degree, he avidly read German literature, philosophy, and—in his own words to a friend—"everything there was in the British Museum" on Whitman. And by his admission

Whitman did a great service to me in making me appreciate the Natural Man and freeing me from much theological or conventional preconceptions [sic] due to my very early pious upbringing. It was a sort of liberation, as St. Paul was liberated from the Law and its damnations by his Damascus vision. Sin ceased to dominate my view of life, and this was a great release as I was inclined to be severely puritanical in all things.[2]

There is no record of when Smuts was first attracted to the study of Whitman, though he had written an essay at Cambridge in 1892 on science and philosophy, an essay that is clearly preparatory to his Whitman study, which is itself a preliminary treatise to his *Inquiry into the Whole* (1911) and the subsequent *Holism and Evolution* (1926). Fundamental to his investigation of *Eenheid* was concern over the antithesis of science and personality, and the way in which Whitman, more than anyone else excepting, perhaps, only Shelley and Goethe, served to synthesize these disparate forces.

In his biography of Smuts, Sir Keith Hancock writes enlighteningly of Smuts's encounter with Whitman:

The deeper he delved into Whitman in those months of 1894 and 1895 the deeper his conviction grew that Whitman and he were kindred spirits. He discovered affinities of ancestry and upbringing: Whitman had had Dutch blood in his veins as well as English— a mixture of sober strains conducive to democratic realism and "devotion to the common and even commonplace"—but Whitman's mother, like his own mother, was not at all commonplace; she was a woman of rare spiritual sensitivity, who lived her life in the "inner light" of Quaker experience. (Could Smuts have foreseen the time when he himself, like Whitman in his later years, would share this experience, or something akin to it?) Whitman, like himself, was deeply influenced in his early childhood by the splendour of his natural surroundings—alas, not the mountains; but in their stead the ocean: Smuts imagined Whitman growing upon the shores of Long Island like Heraclitus on the shores of Asia Minor.[3]

Sometime before the middle of May 1895, Smuts submitted his 70,000-word manuscript to Chapman and Hall, Ltd., publishers. The reader was George Meredith, who recommended against publication. Oswald Crawford, the manager of the publishing house, commented in his letter of rejection (16 May 1895) that the book "is full of thought clearly and well expressed, but at the present moment Walt Whitman is so little considered in this country that I fear, from a commercial point of view, we must regretfully decline your book."[4] He concluded by commending "the sound and safe teaching" which the manuscript contained.

Two days later the author wrote from the Common Room at

Middle Temple to Longmans, Green and Co., offering the "booklet" for publication and describing its content, method, and purpose:

The idea of the work is briefly this. It is an attempt to apply the method of evolution *synthetically* to the study of man. For this purpose I introduce a new conception of "personality" which is developed in chapter I. This "personality" is assumed to develop like any other organism; and this assumption enables the student to state the entire mental life of an individual—including all his ideas and opinions—in terms of the evolution of this personality.

In chapter II I investigate and arrive at the particular "form" of Whitman's personality, and in the remaining chapters I trace as rigorously as possible the development of this personality. In this connection I discuss many of the most important problems of modern thought—such as naturalism, spiritualism, mysticism; the idea of the whole, the cosmic faith, the idea of God, democracy, the future literature of democracy, etc.—as phrases and products of the evolving personality.

You will perhaps ask why I took Whitman, who is certainly not popular in this country. I took him, not only because his is perhaps the most difficult personality that could be taken and thus supplies a very severe test of my general theory, but because his life and work raise so many of the great questions which surround personal evolution.[5]

There is no record of Longmans's reaction to the book, but it can be inferred from the author's offering the manuscript, for either serial or partial publication, to the editor of *Nineteenth Century* on 11 September, shortly after his return to Cape Town. His covering letter indicates his special attachment to the last two chapters which, he hoped, would encourage a widespread appreciation for the idea of the whole "as a key to the vexed problems of ethics, theology, democracy, etc.," and as "the nucleus round which the spiritual thought of the immediate future will probably crystalise." Further, he expressed the hope that his work might "serve to rehabilitate the reputation of one of the most large-minded and spiritual natures; a man withal of keen prophetic insight, whose merits have been obscured by his eccentricities." [6] But *Ninetenth Century* did not publish any part of the manuscript.

The apparent lack of interest in Whitman in England as late as 1895 is hard to understand and explain. By that time, a quantity of serious literary criticism devoted to *Leaves of Grass* had appeared in European journals, though much of it was concerned with the explication of single sections rather than attempting a comprehensive elucidation and evaluation; and there was certainly nothing approaching Smuts's attempt at a psychological and philosophical biography of Whitman. Just as the European studies, in many cases, established precedents in interpretation of individual works, so Smuts's study could well have established a significant precedent had it been published when first submitted. So the anomaly remains: Whitman was the subject of critical analysis and appraisal in Europe, but largely ignored in England.

Even in the remote colonies there was a lively interest in Whitman. In New Zealand he inspired monographs by Mr. and Mrs. William H. Trimble, who also contributed brief essays on *Leaves of Grass* to local periodicals and undertook the compilation of the first concordance to *Leaves of Grass*. (Unpublished, the manuscript is in the library of Brown University.) In Australia the librarian of the Supreme Court of the State of Victoria, Bernard O'Dowd (himself a poet of some stature), established a correspondence with Whitman that continued from August 1889 until Whitman's death. O'Dowd gave public lectures on Whitman and his work, founded a lyceum group for the study of *Leaves of Grass,* and generally acted as promoter and disciple of Whitman. Even John le Gay Brereton, subsequently professor of English in the University of Sydney, published an article, "Hints on Walt Whitman's *Leaves of Grass,*" in the university magazine in 1894. In fact, there is clear evidence of reasonably widespread and erudite interest in Whitman in both Australia and New Zealand by 1895.

In South Africa, however, the situation was much as it was in England. Although the white population there has always exceeded that of New Zealand, where at least five studies of

Whitman (and obituary notices as well) were published before 1900, no record can be found of any article on Whitman before 1960, when two scholarly appreciations were published. Under these circumstances Smuts's deep interest in and understanding of Whitman is the more remarkable and commendable. Lacking stimulation in South Africa and finding discouragement in England, it is amazing that he persisted in his study of Whitman.

After the Boer War, when Smuts returned to Pretoria to reoccupy his rifled house and to resume his law practice, he wrote to his wife, who had remained in Pietermaritzburg convalescing after an operation:

I have got my papers back from Roos, but I do not find the manuscript of *Walt Whitman* among them. Have you any idea where it is? I have so far forgotten to ask Jim; I also do not know if he is acquainted with the manuscript. I shall nonetheless ask him. My law manuscripts are all safe.[7]

This indication of priorities is in itself of interest: the lawyer readying his affairs in preparation for a resumption of his practice is apprehensive for the safety of his manuscript on the American poet about whom nobody in South Africa appears the least concerned!

There is no record of the date or circumstances of the recovery of the manuscript, but the Smuts archives, at present in the Jagger Library of the University of Cape Town and soon to be transferred to the State Library in Pretoria, have both the holograph draft and a manuscript fair copy, impeccably executed by Smuts's wife, Ise, with holograph emendations.

Though the manuscript was never published, knowledge of its existence was widespread, and it was alluded to in Gay Wilson Allen's *Walt Whitman Handbook* (1957) and *Walt Whitman Abroad* (1955), and in biographical studies, so that it has achieved a degree of fame even in its obscurity. Naturally, there have been some attempts at précis, but these have not been entirely satisfactory because of their emphasis on Smuts's method rather than on his substance and conclusions. To

Smuts himself, the originality of his study lay precisely in his approach to Whitman: in seeing *all* of the "good gray poet's" work as the unified, continuous unfolding of a single philosophical statement rather than as a congeries of discrete statements in prose or poetry, over an extended period, and revealing changes from time to time. Smuts saw Whitman's work as a forty-year continuum rather than as the products of forty years. And in a sense he refuted Poe's classic dictum that there was no such thing as a long poem by averring that Whitman's *oeuvre,* whether in prose or poetry, was really an organic and complete composition.

Smuts's son, commenting on *Walt Whitman* in his excellent and enlightening biography of his father, wrote:

The angle of approach to the subject was a new one and the concept not dissimilar to that which brought fame later to Sigmund Freud. But it differs from the textbook psychoanalysts in that it does not split personality into the conscious, subconscious, and so on, but considers it as one integrated whole. This conception of wholes was to mature slowly in his mind and thirty years later appear in his book, *Holism and Evolution.*[8]

Further, he writes that almost forty years after *Walt Whitman* had been written, the author perused much of it and passed a rather perspicacious, though perhaps too stern, judgment on it:

He was much interested in what he read, remarking, "I have read some of the chapters again, and not without amazement. It is full of puerility, but it has remarkable stuff, as coming from a youngster of twenty-four. Indeed, in some respects it is better than *Holism and Evolution.*"[9]

To read the manuscript is to concur in the author's judgment that "it has remarkable stuff," whether from an author of twenty-four or not; and it most assuredly does provide a helpful aid in understanding the philosophy that guided Smuts throughout his lifetime.

Though Whitman could have been replaced by Goethe—the only other "complete personality" of recent history, in Smuts's view—the fact is that he was not, which suggests that, after all, Whitman held a stronger fascination for Smuts than did Goethe. Although he often quoted Goethe in his later years, references to Whitman, and precise quotations, peppered his correspondence throughout the years. Perhaps his most favored lines were from "Faces," which he paraphrased as

> The Lord advances and ever advances,
> Always the shadow in front,
> Always the outstretched Hand
> Helping up the laggards.

Of Smuts's *Walt Whitman,* Hancock writes:

In his book on Whitman he set out to demonstrate a method. Scientists, he said (and here he was going beyond the argument of his Cambridge essay), had been too readily satisfied with the study of origins and of the simpler phenomena in the evolutionary chain: or, if they did sometimes consider the more complex phenomena, they were prone to explain the complex in terms of the simple, "to explain, for instance, human morality and progress by reference to the principles which seem to dominate the animal world." Psychologists, on the other hand, appeared to be victims of an opposite fallacy, for they wrote about mind as if it were a superior and separate entity, as if minds did not belong to persons and persons to the natural world. . . .

In the young Whitman he discovered a "cosmic catholicity", a faculty of "acceptivity" so deeply rooted in the emotional life that it enabled him "to take both sides at the same time", to absorb each separate sensation, to receive each separate idea, although these sensations and ideas contained in their totality contradictions which the conscious intellect would have rejected. In the maturing Whitman he discovered his own zeal for synthesis, his own passionate craving to apprehend and comprehend this puzzling totality as an ordered and harmonious Whole. "I will not make poems in reference to particulars, but I will make poems, songs, thoughts with reference to ensemble." That quotation was from the period which Smuts named "period of naturalism". In Whitman's maturer phase, which he named "period of spiritualism" (perhaps the label did not appear so incongruous then as it does now), he recognised, or believed that he recognised, a deepening apprehension of *en-*

semble, a philosophic vision of "the ultimate harmony of all things"—of Nature; and of Man as belonging to the natural world, but transcending it in his endeavour to understand its laws and to conduct his life within them and beyond them; of Man in quest of Deity.[10]

With so much valuable Whitman criticism now available, one is obliged to place Smuts's book in its historical context fully to appreciate its contribution. In 1895 it was clearly a pioneer study, the more remarkable for having been written by a South African law student, not yet twenty-five.

Smuts's outline of his work, which was presumably prepared in full in advance of composition, bears clear resemblance to a typical lawyer's brief in its detail and logical progression. It enables the reader at a glance to appreciate the structure of the work and to assess its cogency.

Occasionally Smuts is in error in biographical details, but it must be remembered that he was writing just three years after Whitman's death and of necessity had to rely, to a considerable extent, on the hagiographies of R. M. Bucke (*Walt Whitman,* 1883) and John Burroughs (*Notes on Walt Whitman as Poet and Person,* 1867). Both writers uncritically accepted Whitman's own account of his "sound ancestry," general good health, and serenity or imperturbability, and believed that the "I" of the poems invariably carried a personal connotation rather than a universal—that it always referred to Walt Whitman himself and was not the voice of the poet speaking in the *persona* of universal, democratic man. Accordingly, some of Smuts's conclusions bear critical reexamination. But the main tenor of his thesis remains unimpaired, and his pioneering account of the development of Whitman's personality clearly anticipates the directions taken by more recent psychoanalytic criticism.

Biographical assumptions and lacunae have not affected the validity of Smuts's novel value-judgments and appraisals of personality traits or influences that are securely based on his reading of the poems and prose. In this exposition, developing the idea of the whole personality of Whitman, is found his original and principal insight. It permits a corollary: that the develop-

ment of Whitman's personality as a uniquely democratic phenomenon enabled him, more than any poet before him, to give
voice to the soul and aspirations of a democratic society, so that
while "Song of Myself" is supremely Whitman's personal testament, it is at once also the canticle of contemporary civilization, of modern man.

The copy-text for the present edition is the manuscript
written in the hand of Mrs. Smuts and containing the author's
holograph emendations which give it the authority of authorial
revision, together with a Preface that was clearly the product of
later years.

Most of the quotations in the manuscript have marginal page
references to the 1892 editions of *Leaves of Grass* and *Prose
Works;* these have been changed to footnote references to the
now "standard" edition, *The Collected Writings of Walt Whitman,* published by the New York University Press, and un-
identified quotations of significant content or length have been
located and similarly noted. In quoting Whitman, Smuts took
numerous liberties; he changed spelling, capitalization, and
punctuation somewhat capriciously, so that the quoted material
represents an amalgam of British and American usage, with
Whitman's idiosyncratic style seldom preserved. Line-divisions
were frequently not retained from the 1892 text. Smuts's own
practice with respect to spelling and punctuation represented a
confluence of both usages and he revealed a predilection for excessive and unnecessary capitalization. These have been made to
conform to his customary British usage, and capitalization has
been reduced to the minimum necessary, such as to preserve
subtle distinctions in philosophical contexts. Otherwise, editorial changes have been restricted to the restoration of lines of
text dropped, it seems clear, by inadvertence; the correction of
some references; emendation of transposed letters and similar
errors of the amanuensis.

It is a pleasure to acknowledge the kindness of Mr. J. C.
Smuts in authorizing this edition of his father's manuscript;

of the staff of the Firestone Library, Princeton University, in assisting to resolve numerous editorial details; of Cambridge University Press for permitting the inclusion of excerpts from W. K. Hancock's *Smuts: The Sanguine Years, 1870–1919* and from *Selections from the Smuts Papers,* edited by Jean van der Poel and W. K. Hancock; of William Morrow and Co. for permitting the inclusion of excerpts from J. C. Smuts's *Jan Christian Smuts: A Biography;* and of Mrs. Monica Raulf, who typed the manuscript.

Preface

THE PURPOSE and general theory of the following booklet are fully set forth in the first chapter; so that, in regard to them, nothing need be said here.

There is, however, a certain dualism running through the work which may raise difficulties for some readers, and therefore makes it necessary to say a few words of explanation in advance.

The subject of this study is Walt Whitman; but my account does not, so far as I am aware, proceed on the lines which have been generally followed in previous studies, either of Whitman or any other literary thinker. Whitman is here studied from the point of view of the personality and its evolution; the underlying object of the study being to see how far the particular theory of personality here advanced will work in practice. Consequently, the work is addressed to two classes of readers: to those who are generally interested in the work or personality of Whitman, and to those who are interested in a general philosophic theory of the personality. To both classes I wish to say a few words.

The general reader I would beg not to be discouraged by the apparent abstruseness of Chapter 1 or the generality of Chapter 2. If he succeeds in seeing generally what I mean in Chapter 1 by the personality and its "form", and in Chapter 2 by the form of Whitman's personality, he will undoubtedly be in a better position to understand some of the interesting problems discussed in later chapters, and the organic harmony of Whitman's mental development.

The philosophic student will perhaps object that so little theory or philosophy has been introduced into this work. He would perhaps like to see a clear statement of the *general* significance of every part of Whitman's development, and may be disappointed to find that I have largely refrained from generalisation. Originally I had intended to introduce much more theoretical discussion into this study than I actually did introduce afterwards. But on consideration it has seemed advisable to confine the study to a plain statement of my point of view, and of Whitman's mental evolution from that point of view, without considering the general application of the results following from the course and character of that evolution.

Should the underlying theory of this booklet prove correct, and some of the principal features of Whitman's mental development be found to be capable of a general application, it seems to me that very important consequences will follow, which will probably throw a new light on some of the darkest problems of life and thought. If time should ever permit, and it be advisable in other respects, I hope some day to follow up this study of a particular case with a treatment of the general theory of personality in its application to philosophy, ethics, theology, and kindred subjects.

If it is thought that some of the earlier chapters are not so clear and definite as might be wished, I need only remind the reader that any explanation of Whitman's ideas at any period was strictly limited by the evidence belonging to that period; and that the evidence was not always as decisive as I could wish. Besides, the book purports to be an organic whole; and it is impossible to see the exact and full bearing of any one chapter before having read through the whole work.

The booklet was written partly in 1894, while I was still an undergraduate at Cambridge, and partly during the first half of 1895. Originally written for my own amusement and training, I have latterly come to think that it may, if published, benefit from the criticism or development of its fundamental theory at the hands of those who are far more competent than myself to write on such subjects.

Introduction

SCARCELY THREE years have passed since the death of this strange product of American life and activity, and already a considerable library has gathered round his person and writings. And no wonder, for among the remarkable men whom the nineteenth century has produced, Whitman is by no means the least noteworthy, while in some respect his significance is comparable to that of his greatest contemporaries. The very fact that he alone among the writers of our age has tried, however imperfectly, to give utterance to that vast and voiceless spirit of American democracy, to those new aspirations of political and social life with which the rise of the United States in this century is associated, gives him a special significance. When to this striving on his part is added the fact that more than any other writer of his time he was qualified for this work by his vastness and fertility of conception and daring originality of thought and expression, it becomes evident why his character and work have been so hotly canvassed and why more than any other of his literary contemporaries in America he will continue to engage the serious attention of students and thinkers. How far he has successfully gauged and expressed the spirit of America and American civilisation, the future alone can adequately answer; and his work, therefore, whatever judgment may be passed thereon, is always entitled on account of its scope and character to appeal to the bar of posterity, the verdict of which I shall not attempt to anticipate.

It is, however, not so much as the exponent of the American spirit in literature of a high order that Walt Whitman claimed our attention here. It is more on account of his personality and the relation of his work to his personality that he seems to me

to be entitled to a place among the foremost men of the nineteenth century. He was that rarest flowering of humanity—a
true personality, strong, original, organic; a type to which his
fellows could but approximate; a whole and sound piece of
manhood such as appears but seldom, even in the course of
centuries. And it is to such men that we turn our attention
more eagerly and closely, men who do not excel in this or that
special quality or department, but who excel *as men;* in whom
Nature puts forth her highest effort to produce a harmonious
whole, blending qualities which in other men are either wanting or arranged in hostile array. The work of such personalities is not the product of this or that faculty of theirs, but is
the voice of their whole and harmonious manhood, and has
therefore a unique significance for their fellows. And just as
Goethe's lifelong effort was to express his personality and its
developing phases as faithfully as possible in his work, so too
(in a less artistic way, but with perhaps greater fidelity) has
Whitman sought to make his writings as faithful a transcript of
his mind and life as possible. *Leaves of Grass* and his other
works exhibit to us his personality in all its extravagances, ir-
regularities, its weakness and power; we see him in his life
among men and women, and in his loneliness; in strength and
maturity; in weakness and decay. His virtues and his vices are
written down with the same unflinching fidelity. He enables us
to enter behind the curtains of his experience. We pass the
ropes and pulleys and stage-apparatus (of which there is not
much in his case). We take up our position in the innermost
recesses of his personality; and from there we can survey the
whole stage; we can see the engines, the motive-powers, the
entire machinery; we can see how everything is moved; and (if
we are patient) we can see the sources and purposes of the
motion. The self-restraint and reticence which gave such dignity
to the Olympian of Weimar are absent from Whitman's work;
and while this circumstance greatly diminishes the value of his
writings from an artistic point of view, it indefinitely increases
their value, considered as "human documents". That Whitman
had a vast poetic endowment has been admitted even by those

who do not count themselves among his admirers. He was aware of his unique opportunities. And yet he was willing to sacrifice any possible reputation to his intense desire to be himself and reveal his real self to the world. Are we not justified, and even bound, by such invincible fidelity to truth and such an apparent sacrifice, to inquire carefully into the nature and value of his self-revelation or egotism, as the case may be?

Besides, Whitman claims to be not only of his age, but also, in the highest sense, above it; the doubts and misgivings which are peculiarly associated with the great scientific and democratic advance of our century have no meaning for him. With the eye of understanding he reads his age; with the eye of faith he surveys its future. In the doubts of his age he sees only the beginning of a vaster faith, the outlines of which he does not hesitate to draw with a bold hand. It may be of interest to trace clearly the growth of his religious ideas and to inquire in how far his pretensions as a seer or prophet are justified.

Finally and especially, Whitman was not only a great personality raised above the cloudy region of doubt into the blue zone of faith, he was a man who only by a long evolution and much painful experience and hard striving attained to that mastery. He was an organic personality developing all his lifetime like a product of nature, travelling through the successive cycles of his growth. He has not only a history of experience, but also of personality. In reading his works the student feels that he is in the biological world. He is not watching the changing colours of some psychological kaleidoscope; he is following the evolution of a personality. The phases are those of a growing organism; the ideas—their form and content—mark the gradations in a soul's development. His mind or personality was organic, and hence his work remains vital and of greatest interest and instructiveness to us.

To trace the bases and fundamental keynotes of his character and personality and to study his work and thought as the organic outcome of that personality is the object of this booklet.

1

Method and Subject

EVOLUTION IS perhaps the most striking—certainly it is
the most telling—instance that could be given of the dynamic
force which an idea is capable of exercising over the thoughts
and opinions of men. Up till the middle of this [the nine-
teenth] century scarcely more than a whim of the philosophers,
it has since then succeeded in all but transforming our entire
conception of the universe and man's relation to it. What the
Copernican theory has done for astronomy; what the New-
tonian dynamic has done for our knowledge of the mechanism
of the physical universe; what the molecular kinetic has done
for our knowledge of the constitution of matter, that the
method or idea of evolution has done and still is doing for our
comprehension of the biological world. That from mightiest
system to tiniest particle all matter is in eternal motion in
obedience to certain supposed forces, that the phenomena of
life—from its lowest to its highest manifestations—are inseparable links in a chain of individual and collective evolution,
such are the ideas that have proved fruitful in our endeavour
to pierce the mystery of our surroundings. Vast and indeed
revolutionary as have been the results of the idea of evolution
so far, it may be confidently asserted that its greatest triumphs
remain still to be won in the field of patient and unflagging re-
search.

It is true that some people of too weak faith or too sanguine temperaments are already beginning to experience the lassitude of reaction. And this reaction is undoubtedly accelerated by the disgust which they feel for an error just the reverse of their own. In proportion as evolution has become an idol in the Baconian—if not the Biblical—sense; in proportion as a sort of halo or sentimental haze has been gathering round the grim scientific conception of Darwin; others have begun to forswear evolution as a will-o'-the-wisp. To some it has become talisman, to others anathema. The latter may sometimes be overheard using such excited language as the following: "Your men of genius, your great thinkers and experimenters, have been applying the evolutionary method to the elucidation of the great problems of society, ethics, religion. What has been the result of all their work? Have they been able to explain how the flower of spontaneous self-sacrifice has bloomed on the blood-stained fields of competition and the struggle to live? Have they been able to explain the nature and sanction of those impalpable sentiments which alone can cement human society? Has this precious method of evolution enabled them to hear and interpret that cry for purity and holiness which, reaching through the loud bawl of sordid interest, rises ever more audibly from the far depths of the human soul as the ages roll on? Has this new telescope focussed more successfully the uncertain rays that visit us from the surrounding and pervading spiritual world? Away with evolution and whatever else justifies selfishness, saps practical morality, drains human life of its spiritual well-springs, and calls the highest incarnations of our ideals mere 'illusions'!"

And yet it seems that the real work of evolution still remains to be done. Its real battles are still to be fought and won in those very departments of biography, society, ethics, and religion in which it seems so far to have been conspicuously unsuccessful.

In fact, it is doubtful whether the method of evolution has ever yet been vigorously applied in the higher ranges of genius, of creative imagination, of transcendent mental and spiritual force. One need only turn to the ordinary books of literary criticism to see that their writers have not yet—except in the vaguest possible sense—apprehended the idea or the method of evolution. The method still adopted by the vast majority of critics in examining the work of great thinkers and artists produces the impression that a man's ideas and opinions are realities separate and separable from him, to be considered as distinct entities apart from the mind that produced them. A man's work is treated not as the vital outcome of a certain mind or personality—to be explained only by reference to that personality and its evolution—but as a congeries of opinions, views, conclusions on things in general. These opinions are then either approved or condemned according to the ethical and artistic standards which the particular critic happens to patronise. As if the product of an organic intelligence is a dogma, a system of opinions, and not rather a life! As if the mind of man is like a herbarium, filled with the dead and dried thought-specimens carefully classified, and not rather a garden in which the inner life-forces manifest themselves in varied and changing forms! So long as such utter disregard of the idea of evolution still prevails, it is perfectly idle to say that its work is done and that the time has come for it to retire gracefully from the scene.

Part of the ill success of evolution in these higher ranges of life is no doubt traceable to the wrong manner in which the idea has been too often applied there. In the first place, there has been too strong a tendency among evolutionists to state the phenomena of the highest regions of biological development in terms of the lower and even the lowest; to explain, for instance, human morality and progress by reference to the principles which seem to dominate the animal world. It is exactly parallel to the mistake, which was formerly made, of interpreting life in terms of force and energy.

Secondly, the application of the idea of evolution has hitherto been too analytic. Evolution is the process in life, both of plants and animals. Now, as life is the most synthetic phenomenon we know, as indeed it is the original source of our idea of synthesis, it follows that the method which professes to explain its phenomena and laws ought to be very largely a synthetic one. The most successful anatomy of the body and the mind will not bring us nearer to the fundamental conception of the life itself which pervades the body and the products of the mind. We do not get at the whole by a careful study and summing up of the parts, for the whole is greater than the sum of its parts. The true life in each individual is that unity which underlies all its manifold manifestations; it is not the sum of those manifestations. And evolution can only become a fruitful method in the study of the higher regions of life when its application becomes largely synthetic; when it is applied to the phenomena of life not only separated and individually, but especially as a whole.

How far has this synthetic character of evolution been recognised in its application to the study, say, of human life? The only important application that has so far been made occurs in the science of psychology.

Now, how far has the application of the evolutionary conception in psychology been synthetic? On looking into the current textbooks on that subject, I find that psychologists first divide the mental or psychic phenomena of human life into the unconscious and the conscious. The unconscious phenomena they set aside as not properly within the scope of their subject. The conscious mental phenomena are then divided into intellect, feeling or emotion, and volition, and these are then separately anatomised in their historical development in the growing individual.

This seems all very ingenious; and the results arrived at are no doubt of importance and interest. But where is the synthesis? My own reading—which I frankly admit to be very limited—has never yet brought me to any treatise which shows, or tries to show, how the mind develops and acts as a whole. In the spacious home of the mind the mistress is never to be seen, but always instead the obtrusive janitor, waiter, and butler! Surely, till some humble corner is accorded to the mind in her own house, evolution has not yet found its true application in psychology. While the analytic application of the evolutionary conception to psychology has led to very important results, far more important results may be anticipated from its synthetic application.

In order to arrive at the startingpoint for this synthetic application, we must first cease to cut up the mind into intellect, feeling, and volition. We must also cease to divide its phenomena into the conscious and the unconscious. Thus we arrive at undifferentiated and unanalysed mental life. What do we gain by ignoring these distinctions? Among others, we gain this: that now for the first time we shall have to study the influence of the unconscious part in our mental life along with that of the conscious part. This unconscious part—the vast region of mental twilight in which the primordial forces of our cosmic nature disport themselves without the interference of the will or the prying of the consciousness—is undoubtedly very important, if not the most important part of our inner life.

Thus, then we arrive at the life of the individual so far as it has effects in the department of mind. By studying mental life as a whole—including both the conscious and the unconscious factors in it—we shall soon get beyond the range of the pure psychological. It is sometimes said that the historical study of mind is either psychology or nothing. I think it is evident from what has just been said that the synthetic study of mind —involving as it does factors which psychology ignores—will expose the error lurking in this dictum.

Two questions now suggest themselves: First, what is the best or the true startingpoint for the synthetic evolutionary study of mental phenomena? Second, what is the practical method to be adopted in such a study?

The general answer to the first question is evident. The mental life, considered as a whole, is the startingpoint for the synthetic study of mental growth. But this answer is in itself too vague to be of any practical use. Let us, therefore, examine it more closely.

What is the most fundamental and characteristic property of all life—both in plants and animals? It seems to be the property of developing, growing, or evolving from within, from itself, and of reorganising all nutritive material according to its own inner requirements. The process by which life maintains and develops itself is not merely mechanical, it is not even merely chemical. Behind the assimilative chemistry of any form of life lies that mysterious force which determines the nature of the chemical and mechanical processes by which life is nourished. And every form of life, every plant and animal, is a centre of such peculiar transforming power, in accordance with its own requirements. Every individual case of life seems to say to itself as follows: "I am small, but I have an irrepressible desire to become great—as great as it is possible for me to become. I am going to use whatever means I am capable of using to forward this greatness of myself. But I vow that it will be and remain in the deepest sense of my own greatness. Not the material I use, nor the aids, will build up my greatness. I am going to do everything myself, and in my own way, and for my own pleasure". This property of growing from itself, in itself, and for itself, seems to be the most fundamental of life, and is as characteristic of the highest form, Man, as of the lowest forms.

Now, from this fundamental property of universal life follow two conclusions of paramount importance:

(1) Every individual form of life is a unity, a centre of activity dominated by one fundamental property. It is this ultimate internal unity that shapes the innumerable products of life into an orderly and harmonious whole.

(2) In every individual form of life this fundamental property operates according to its own inherent laws and forms. It may be, of course, that several forms of life are similar; so similar as to be indistinguishable. But even then it is impossible for them to be the same. Plant A may be perfectly similar to plant B; but they are nevertheless two plants, each with its own fundamental laws or forms of growth. These laws or forms may be perfectly similar, but they are as perfectly distinct in the two cases. The only difference between the two perfectly similar plants will be that of being or life: the same in all other respects, they are absolutely distinct in regard to this most fundamental particular.

The foregoing remarks about life being intended to be quite general, apply to the human being. In other words, each human individual is a perfectly distinct entity, animated by a single, indivisible unity of life, whch has its own distinct laws and forms of growth. This distinct, single, indivisible unity of life in each individual I call the personality of that individual.

This conception of personality must not be confused with the "transcendental ego", or *das intelligible Ich* of the metaphysician, nor with the "self-consciousness" of our friend the psychologist. I have already pointed out that this ultimate inner life is largely, if not chiefly, unconscious. And as for the transcendental ego, an obstinate and regrettable stupidity has hitherto prevented me from piercing the metaphysical haze which surrounds that mystery, and makes the literature on the subject a sealed book to me. All that I have been able to gather in a general way is that the personality is rapidly becoming one of the points at which metaphysicians are concentrating their forces and planting their batteries. While cheerfully admitting and even ardently wishing that the metaphysical batteries may yet do serious execution, I have sometimes a suspicion that the elevation of their aim is somewhat too great, and that their projectiles may proceed clean over the mark. Nor is it likely that this regrettable result will be prevented by the lowering influence of gravity on the projectiles, for at the giddy altitude from which they are discharged, the force of gravity must be practically zero. What with this difficulty, and the bewildering smoke which seems to be an inevitable accompaniment of metaphysical warfare, the personality may yet rejoice at a complete escape from the much-vaunted attack. Leaving the absolute consciousness, the transcendental ego, and similar entities *in abstracto* and *sub specia aeternitatis* to those who are competent to deal with them, I return to the physical or biological personality as above indicated.

It has been said that every individual case of life—and therefore also the personality—develops according to its own inherent and fundamental law or laws, which may or may not be similar to the corresponding law or laws of other cases of life.

The term "law" means, in this connection, principle of growth; and as in any case it is unfortunate, I shall now try to get rid of it by substituting a different conception.

There is a certain conception in philosophy which, though usually said to correspond to nothing existing, has yet had an apparently indestructible vitality which invests it with a profound significance. That conception appears in Plato as the "idea" and, it seems, in a very similar form in Aristotle and his followers. It appears in Bacon—the professed enemy of Aristotelianism, and sometimes called the father of modern science —as the "form". It appears also in Hegel—whose philosophical tenets seem to differ considerably from those of Plato, Aristotle, or Bacon—under the guise of the *Idee*. Disguising itself in different shapes, the conception remains yet the same in substance. To the artistic Plato the "idea" is that perfect type of which the things existing in the phenomenal world are but fragments or imperfect reflections. To the scientific Bacon the "form" of anything is that underlying, inherent cause of it which will account fully for its existence, properties, and activities. To the dialectic Hegel the *Idee* of a thing is that immanent activity or life-principle which, in the absence of external interference or impediments, will perfectly realise the potency or capability of that thing; and sometimes the conception shifts from this immanent activity or process to the fully evolved and perfect result. It is obvious that if the personal element is eliminated from these variations, the result in all three will be the same. But the most curious thing about this protean conception— making it one of the most interesting phenomena in the history of philosophy—is the fact that such sane masterminds should have staked their philosophic reputations on something which is alleged to be non-existent. The common-sense Bacon, in particular, makes the existence of "forms" the very basis of his theory of induction, the new organon which—in his belief— was to revolutionise knowledge.

I should submit that the thing corresponding to the conception does really exist in one case; and that the conception has been extended by analogy to other cases. *The conception is a self-intuition; is the reflection in the mind of the nature of the personality.* These profound spirits, probing their own thoughts in order to find some typical truth or idea which might assist them in compassing and coordinating the vast universe of phenomena, found in their consciousness the reflection of the one thing of which they and all have the deepest knowledge and experience; namely, the self. That is, so far, a truism. But further: they also saw (I assume and submit) in that reflection the very nature and essence of the personality. If this assumption is correct, we see that there is in the personality a characteristic activity—distinct in each individual—of the immanent life, the unrestrained and natural development of which will realise the full promise and potency of that life. This characteristic activity or capacity I shall call the *form of the personality*. The form of the personality is thus the Hegelian *Idee* inherent in the personality; it is that special and characteristic activity of the life in each individual which contains both the limits and capabilities of the individual growth, and whose uninterrupted operation will exhaust the capabilities of that personality. This form of the personality resembles closely the idea of fate. It is an immanent fate operating in every individual, which can be thwarted, but never fundamentally altered, by circumstances. The form is primordial and immutable, but its full development can be retarded or stopped in some respects or other by sufficiently powerful external factors. It is also distinct and more or less different in all men.

This conception of the personality is professedly an assumption; but it cannot be considered a violent one.[1] The following chapters are written with a view principally to testing the actual working-value of this conception in one particular case.

For this purpose a certain individual will be selected. An attempt will be made to arrive at the form of his personality—the fundamental characteristic of his mental constitution. Then an attempt will be made to show how this form, under the unfolding influence of his experience, and in coalescence with elements furnished by that experience, produced the ideas of his maturity. Finally, the gradual modifications which these ideas underwent during the later periods of his development will be traced. This booklet is thus an attempt to arrive at the ultimate form of some individual personality, and then to deduce its entire mental evolution from, and express it in terms of, this form of the personality and its evolution.

It will thus be seen that, difficult as is my task, it is in fact merely an attempt to thoroughly test what I consider to be the fundamental conception of the personality. I cherish the hope —not without some cause—that the conception is fraught with far-reaching results for philosophy, ethics, religion, etc. But the consideration of these larger issues falls largely beyond the range of the present unpretending little work.

Such being the startingpoint for a synthetic application of evolution to the study of mind, what is to be the practical method of that study? It is the objective method. The records of the individual's life and work and development are carefully examined with a due regard especially to dates; and from such evidence the general laws and results of his evolution are stated. The form of his personality furnishes the germ-plasm of the mind; its actual evolution must be traced by a full historical examination and induction. It will thus be seen that I propose to treat the subject of personality from a biological point of view, and exactly as any individual plant or animal might be treated. The method and ultimate assumptions will be practically the same, though the results may be poles asunder.

The next point is to decide on a suitable individual on whom to test the practical value of the conception. Now biological phenomena are generally best studied in the most perfect and fully developed specimens. Our patient must consequently have a well-marked personality and a striking capacity for development. Even strongly-marked personalities vary in the character and range of their development. In some the assimilative and reorganising power of the personality is much more conspicuous than in others; in a third class the range of development is very small.

The last class includes the (perhaps) exceptional cases of arrested development or early maturity. Carlyle may be taken as a typical instance of it. He wrote *Sartor Resartus* in early manhood; he continued to write to an extreme old age. Yet one who reads through all the volumes of Carlyle ultimately comes to the conclusion that in *Sartor Resartus* his ideas had almost reached the stage of finality. In his later works he repeated those ideas; he applied them in different departments of history; he applied them in the criticism of contemporary life, thought, politics. But there was almost no observable development in them. The X's, Y's, Z's of the formulae, in which he summed up the results of his thinking on the great problems of life, and the tendencies of the modern world, were solved in early manhood; since then they had remained constant, invariable in form and almost invariable in meaning. His temper became a little more irritable; his attitude a little more dogmatic; perhaps he hankered, or his theories made him hanker, a little more after the "great man". But his fundamental ideas remained practically the same.

Of the class of imperfect assimilative capacity Tennyson may serve as a specimen. A careful perusal of his works in their chronological order certainly produces the impression that there was considerable development in his mental activity. But it is impossible to attribute the change in his work to an organic development of his mind. The changing phases of his work mark not the growth of a personality, but the reflex of certain phases of his times. Such development as there is in his work is not so much the outcome of an internal, organic growth of his mind, as of an infusion *ab extra* of the thoughts current in his generation. The man does not so much mould the experience, as the experience dominates the man.

Goethe is a type of the first class—of the men who have a history, not only of experience, but also of personality. In reading his works the student feels that he is in the biological world. He is not watching the changing colours of some psychological kaleidoscope; he is following the evolution of a personality. The phases are those of a growing organism; the ideas—their form and content—mark the gradations in a soul's evolution. Goethe's experience was thoroughly assimilated and transformed according to the form of his personality. His mind was organic, his work remains vital.

In order to study the evolution of the personality in the most instructive way, our subject must be selected from the last-mentioned class; must be, like Goethe, an organic, developing personality. Besides this, the main purpose of his life must have been his own personal evolution. In men who have devoted their powers to the attainment of some other end—such as some great scientific or political achievement—the personality may be just as well-marked and evolutionary, but it cannot in their case be studied under the same favourable conditions.

Considering all these requisites, I have found my choice practically limited to two men: Goethe and Walt Whitman; and I have selected the latter. In many respects Goethe appeared to me an ideal personality for a subject: vast in range of power and development; massive; profound; while his main ideas have now for almost a century been leavening the world's thought. And Goethe has this additional advantage, that his life is perhaps better known than that of any other man that ever lived. But the Goethe literature has grown to such incompassable dimensions that its accurate study must be the work of a laborious lifetime.

On the other hand, Whitman's work is confined within narrow limits, comparatively. Besides, Whitman presents enormous difficulties; and if the method of personality enables us to surmount them with more or less success, that will be the best test of its practical value. It has often been remarked by those even who have studied Whitman most seriously and successfully that his work is confused and incapable of reduction to order or system. That his work is apparently confused, and that it is often as difficult to understand as it is important and fascinating, in part strikes every sympathetic reader at the first glance into *Leaves of Grass*. Whitman himself knew this, and has given characteristic expression to it in one of his earliest pieces:

No dainty dolce affettuoso I,
Bearded, sun-burnt, grey-neck'd, forbidding, I have arrived,
To be wrestled with as I pass for the solid prizes of the universe,
For such I afford whoever can persevere to win them.[2]

If the root-conception of personality enables us to arrive at a point of view from which it will be possible to see the organic and biological, if not the logical, harmony of his work, it will have done much to recommend itself to general acceptance.

Lastly, Whitman has this supreme claim to be the subject of a sketch like this—that he has tried more carefully and persistently, and perhaps successfully, and probably at a greater sacrifice than any other writer, to make his work as faithful a transcript of his own mind and growth as possible. *Leaves of Grass* and his other works exhibit to us his personality in all its extravagances, regularities, its weakness and power; we see him in his life among men and women, and in his loneliness; in strength and maturity; in weakness and decay; his virtues and his vices are written down with the same unflinching fidelity. He enables us to enter behind the curtains of his experience. We pass the ropes and pulleys and stage-apparatus (of which there is not much in his case). We take up our position in the innermost recesses of his personality; and from there we can survey the whole stage; we can see the engines, the motive-powers, the entire machinery; we can see how everything is moved; and (if we are patient) we can see the sources and purposes of the motion. The self-restraint and reticence which gave such dignity to the Olympian of Weimar are absent from Whitman's work; and while this circumstance greatly diminishes the value of his writings from an artistic point of view, it indefinitely increases their value, considered as "human documents". That Whitman had a vast poetic endowment has been admitted even by those who do not count themselves among his admirers. He was aware of his unique opportunities. And yet he was willing to sacrifice any possible reputation to his intense desire to be himself and reveal his real self to the world. Are we not justified, and even bound, by such invincible fidelity to truth and such an apparent sacrifice, to inquire carefully into the nature and value of his self-revelation or egotism, as the case may be?

2

The Form of
Whitman's Personality

IN THE Orphic philosophy, it seems that a distinction was drawn between δαιμων and τυχή—δαιμων referring to the original capacity of the individual, which experience could call forth, but not materially change; τυχή referring to the moulding effect of experience on the original capacity. The latter is the acquired element in human character; the former is the innate or connate element, to use the terminology of the schools. The distinction, notwithstanding its metaphysical abuse, is yet a profoundly true one. There is in every human being that irreducible residuum of individual identity which no acquired experience will account for. No accidents of experience, no combination of coincidences, no grinding operation of the iron laws of social assimilation, operating through the individual life, can produce or destroy that primordial personality or can efface that original impress or capacity of selfhood with which every man is born into the world.

> *Und keine Zeit und keine Macht zerstückelt*
> *Geprägte Form, die lebend sich entwickelt.*[1]

Taking this distinction for granted, without attempting to explore its metaphysical or biological basis, we ask next: What was this primordial personality of Whitman? If this can be found, we shall have a clue to guide us through many a dark labyrinth in his work and enable us to see the harmony that pervades the whole.

Spiritualism

Whitman had not the intellectual type of mind. Though a man who operated with such great ideas as he has done, covering the whole range of ethical, social, and political life, must needs have had an intelligence of a very high order, yet in him the intellect was second and subservient to other faculties of the mind.

The power of the intellect is measured by the clearness and distinctness with which it conceives ideas, by the sharpness of outline which it draws round its somewhat intangible concepts, or by its power of keeping those concepts distinct and separate from the nebulous thought-elements that surround them. The intellect thus narrows, concentrates, divides.

On the other hand, the emotional faculty, more especially in its sympathetic activities, is like the oil that flows softly yet irresistibly round an object, filling up cavities and slowly effecting an entrance into the object. It is like a liquid that ceaselessly saps the permanence of a solid and tries, by dissolving it, to establish uniformity between it and its environment. Thus, while the intellect is hard and rigid, the emotional faculty is soft, plastic; and reconciles, levels, equalises.

In Whitman the emotional faculty predominated distinctly over the intellectual. His mind was fluid and sympathetic. It did not so much distinguish and differentiate as try to wash away all distinctions and differences. It did not proceed logically to its conclusions; it did not ascend step by step the logical ladder which leads from the particular to the general, from the singular to the universal. It throbbed forward on the waves of its own irresistible impulse. Its path was not marked by the fixed points, the logical rests, by which the reasoning faculty moves forward. Its vehicle was rather the impalpable ether of sentiment that bathes for ever the personality. It was not any scientific induction, but his sympathetic insight which, operat-

43

ing on the extensive materials of his experience, prompted to him his main ideas.

But the activity of this emotional faculty is different in different men. In Whitman the object and scope of the emotional faculty was—as will shortly appear—the universal. There was nothing sectional, narrow, parochial about his sympathies. With the soul and the temperament of an enthusiast, he combined that universality of outlook which made him one of the sanest of men. Further, as this magnitude of mental life and interest prevented the activity of his sympathies from crystallizing in any particular direction, the emotional faculty in him retained that flexibility, that fluidity, which permeated all his ideas. He seems to have felt more than any other man the currents and cross-currents that circulate through the personality; the invisible forces which sustain, or rather form, mental life. What wonder that he came to view the entire physical, biological, and spiritual universe as an aggregate of such inscrutable forces; and the phenomena of life and existence as but moments in the eternally progressive manifestation of the world-energy! To the intense gaze of his emotional insight all the old landmarks which philosophy and politics, society and morality, have established, are washed away; the waters are once more covering the earth, and over the face of the waters is once more brooding the Divine Spirit. It is not so much the constituted forms as the underlying and shaping forces that he regards. It is the ebb and flow, the coming and going, in the currents of the physical and moral world that fascinated him more than its stability or permanence.

This "flux" philosophy is, of course, at least as old as Heraclitus. In Whitman these ideas don't assume the form of a technical system of philosophy. They are rather the vital outcome of his total personality. And it is this that distinguishes him from the philosophers. The processes of existence are with him not a deduction from abstract ideas; they are the expression of his own personality. His flux universe is the projection of his own flux personality on the dark screen of the objective.

The gradual evolution of this emotional, ideal, spiritual flux element in his mind, as shown in his conceptions of personality, society, ethics, cosmology, and religion, will be traced in due course.

Realism

If this emotional, dynamic element in his mind had been unbalanced by some other equally strong element, it is pretty easy to predict what he might possibly have become. If his mind had led him to abstract speculation, he would have been another of those ontological philosophers who lose themselves groping in the labyrinth of being and knowing. If he had taken to religion, he would have been a rapt mystic; if to politics, he would have. been an anarchist or other unpractical enthusiast. How is it that, while having the capacity for all these developments in him, he never became a philosopher, or mystic, or anarchist, and never pioneered the forlorn hope of any enthusiasm?

This brings us to the other grand characteristic of his mental constitution. This is his sense of reality, his grip of actual fact, his extraordinary hold on the objective. And here again we have to do not with any mere abstract idea, any adventitious conception of the intellect, but with a constituent element of the whole man. To some men (e.g., Shelley) this world is a passing shadow and a dream in a more than merely metaphorical sense; they are destitute almost altogether of the sense of reality. At the opposite pole of mental habit we have the majority of mankind, who look upon the objective world very much as Peter Bell [2] regarded a primrose: to him it was a yellow primrose and no more. Between these two extremes there are many types of mind; and Whitman's was one of these. The idea, the sense of the reality of the world had in him risen to self-consciousness, so to speak. While his insight pierced through the shows and forms of things, the realistic intensity of his nature filled those things with something more real than ordinary reality. He possessed in a unique degree that precious gift, so rare among great thinkers, the sense of the concrete.

The tendency for the thinker is to translate the concrete into the abstract; to resolve the actualities of the external world into abstractions; and then, forgetting that the abstract is merely a translation, to mistake it for the original; to transform the mysterious manuscript of the concrete into a palimpsest and write over it the garbled version of the abstract.

Now this sense of the concrete-real Whitman possessed, and he had all that the possession of this sense implies. The freshness and directness of his language, the unique accuracy of his epithets and descriptions of natural objects—all bear testimony to his patient scrutiny of the concrete thing. To him there was reality not only in force, in energy, in spirit (which philosophers generally believe in), but also in matter—poor, despised, discredited matter. In his philosophy of life, hunger occupies a place side by side with love; the material side by side with the mental and spiritual affinities of human nature.

The influence of this realistic element in Whitman's mind will be traced later on. Only one important aspect of it must be mentioned here. He was not content to live in a world of ideas and ideals; he was passionately bent on realising them. He was not satisfied with opening to democracy the vista of a great future, with bringing before his country some of the great ideas that make for its future happiness and peace. He realised those ideas in himself; he incorporated them into his personality. This achievement is unique; but the type of man that sets himself such an achievement as one of the great tasks of his life is equally unique.

There are men whose thoughts in the deepest sense never became parts of their personalities. Perhaps Shakespeare is an instance of the very highest order of intelligence in which there was this divorce between the inner and the outer life; between the intelligence and the personality. His great mental characteristic seems to have been imagination. "Fancy's child", Milton calls him with profound truth. With the magic wand of the creative imagination he could body forth an ideal world in which his vast mental energies found full scope; but in that imaginary world they remained. Even the sonnets may be a product of his imagination, with only a very scanty basis of fact to support their imaginary ardours. Shakespeare never heard the imperious inner call towards self-realisation; and outwardly he remained that kindly, witty, "gentle Will Shakspere" that his associates took him to be, while inwardly his mind was really traversing the whole orbit of human experience. His development was on the plane of the imagination, not of reality.

On the other hand, some men there are who not only enrich literature with new thoughts, but who also become living embodiments of their highest and best ideas. Goethe, laboriously building up the "pyramid of his existence" by realising in his life-experience the larger and wider ideas which he had conceived, and Whitman, rearing himself into a monument of American manhood to prove what the democratic ideal could do for the individual, are perhaps the best modern instances of men who have enlarged the area, not only of human ideals, but also of realisation of those ideals.

Receptivity and Acceptivity

While the realistic and idealistic tendencies in Whitman's personality are *prima facie* original or incapable of reduction to more primordial elements, the third—and no less striking—tendency in his mental constitution seems to be derivative, to be merely an aspect of his vast, sympathetic emotionality. This is his unique receptivity, his remarkable avidity for experience and his capacity for absorbing the materials of his experience.[3]

Many of the world's great personalities are remarkable for their self-centredness; for their independence, to a large extent, of the materials of experience. With some it is certain great ideas of the intellect, with others it is certain great intuitions of the soul, that occupy and fill almost exclusively the entire field of attention. Such experience as they have seems to serve but as the motive power which sets the whole machinery of mental activity into operation.

With Whitman it was otherwise; his receptive power was abnormal, and has struck some as his most distinctive quality.

Whether his mental power was equal to the task of coordinating and dominating his vast experience; whether his genius was intense enough to fuse and transform this amorphous experience into those clear forms that last forever in literature and art, may perhaps seem doubtful. There can be no doubt about the immense range of his physical and social experience, and the insatiable avidity he evinced throughout life to acquire more.

One remarkable phase of this receptivity must be referred to, as it pervades so generally the work of Whitman as to strike even the superficial reader. This form of his receptive capacity may be called *acceptivity*. This is his power of assenting to or acquiescing in the apparent opposite of what he had assented to only a moment before. Ordinary mortals generally take sides, not only in religion and politics, but also in almost everything else, real or imaginary. If they like A, they almost inevitably dislike or disapprove of the not-A. Far different is it with this all-embracing cosmopolitan or universalist. He refuses generally to take sides, and when he does, it is with both the opposing parties before him. And he has a faculty of taking both sides at the same time and with equal passion—which is very disconcerting to the ordinary reader. It is not indifference or cynicism which makes him thus impartial or catholic. This cosmic catholicity is rather the product of his all-absorptive capacity and of his power of merging all distinctions, which have been mentioned already as a phase of his sympathetic emotionality. It is, in short, not disdainful superiority or indifference, but acceptivity.

Here, then, we have the three most general characteristics of Whitman's mind—spiritualism, realism, and acceptivity. But I have already shown that receptivity was only a form or phase of his spiritualism. Thus the only fundamental characteristics left are spiritualism and realism; and the combination of these two forms the basis of Whitman's mind.

This is the most rare combination; but it is the combination that undoubtedly existed in Whitman. Some few men have the emotional, spiritual, soaring power in a supreme degree. But they lack a sense of reality, an eye for the material, the concrete.

Others again are intensely practical; they feel, and feel truly, that the world is no mere phantasmagory; that the world is real and solid, and the source of all reality and solidity in man's unstable thought. But their minds lack wings; they cannot soar into that higher world of the great ideas, where alone the human mind can mew its mighty youth. Whitman combined in a unique degree both realism and spiritualism.

But can we not proceed still further and reduce this duality of spiritualism and realism in his mental constitution to a fundamental unity? I think we can. It may perhaps be safely said that the fundamental factor in his mind was spiritualism— that dissolving, dynamic, sympathetic emotionality which has been already fully explained. His passion for reality and realisation, for first-hand experience and direct contact with things, was only a mode of the activity of his spiritual tendency. In proportion as the "flux" tendency dissolved for him what seemed fixed and permanent in life and thought; in proportion as it swept away superficial distinctions and forms, and discovered the really operative factors underlying the apparently solid and permanent forms, in that proportion it brought him within the domain of reality and nourished the passion for that reality. While spiritual idealism alienates some minds from this rough world and makes them hanker after the Utopian cloud-lands that lie beyond the borders of this world, on others it has a directly opposite effect. It makes them return to the dark verities of mother Earth; in brooding sympathy and mystic passion they listen ever more attentively to the dark echoes that haunt her mighty soul. And of this latter class was Whitman. Spiritualism rose in him to realism. Or more briefly: the emotional-spiritual capacity of Whitman had two aspects—one was its universalising extensity; the other its realising intensity. Thus, then, we reach the form of Whitman's personality. It is the "flux" form—dynamic, emotional, spiritual; universal in range and realistic in character.

3

Factors in the
Early Evolution of Whitman's
Personality (1819-1850)

Home and Religion

BORN 31 MAY 1819, at West Hills, Long Island, of English and Dutch parentage, Whitman derived from both stocks that practicality and sanity, that devotion to the common and even the commonplace, which distinguish both branches of the Teutonic race. Besides, John Burroughs [1] noted several instances of the spiritual or intuitive temperament among his ancestors; his mother seems from his own account to have been a woman of a deeply religious bent of mind. Heredity would thus account for the presence in him of the remarkable qualities which were noted above. It was their peculiar combination and intensity that distinguished him. Profoundly susceptible to all the subtler and nobler influences of personality, his mind seems to have been most deeply and lastingly impressed by the simple piety of his mother. Whether his parents were Quakers, I have not been able to determine with certainty. They, however, attended the religious services of the Friends, and young Walt often accompanied them. Various allusions scattered through *Leaves of Grass,* and especially the account he wrote of Elias Hicks, the Quaker, to whose sermons he listened as a boy of ten years or thereabouts, show what profound impression these addresses made on his young mind. Whatever its value and extent as a factor in his early development, there can be no doubt that the mystical theory of the "Inner Light", to which reference will again be made in the last chapter, left an indelible impression on his mind.

The Sea

Another very potent influence of his early years, to which his later work bears testimony, is traceable to his early surroundings. The locality in which his parents lived originally was quite rural, and much of his time seems to have been spent by the seaside. The influence of the sea was undoubtedly one of the most important factors in the growth of his thought; subtly and indelibly it coloured all his views in a quite remarkable degree, and was the direct source of some of the most eloquent and suggestive passages in *Leaves of Grass*. Witness, among innumerable others, the little piece called "In Cabin'd Ships at Sea", in which he makes the sailors of some future time compare his fluid poems to the phenomena of sea-life:

Here are our thoughts, voyagers' thoughts,
Here not the land, firm land, alone appears, may then by them be
    said,
The sky o'erarches here, we feel the undulating deck beneath our
    feet,
We feel the long pulsation, ebb and flow of endless motion,
The tones of unseen mystery, the vague and vast suggestions of the
    briny world, the liquid-flowing syllables,
The perfume, the faint creaking of the cordage, the melancholy
    rhythm,
The boundless vista and the horizon far and dim are all here,
And this is ocean's poem.[2]

This almost inexplicable passion for the sea remained with him to the very last. Thus in the late evening of his life he addressed the sea as follows:

The first and last confession of the globe,
Outsurging, muttering from thy soul's abysms,

The tale of cosmic elemental passion,
Thou tellest to a kindred soul.[3]

But indirectly the inspiration of the "briny world" affected all his ideas and in some sense determined his ultimate attitude towards the great issues raised in his mature work. Reference has already been made to the peculiar form which the emotional, fluid temperament assumed in him. The "flux" conception of the universe which Heraclitus arrived at on the shores of Asia Minor, which modern science has arrived at by the more rigorous methods of experimental and mathematical investigation, young Whitman literally imbibed on the shores of Long Island. He himself describes this indirect influence in the following curious passage:

Even as a boy, I had the fancy, the wish, to write a piece, perhaps a poem, about the sea-shore—that suggesting, dividing line, contact, junction, the solid marrying the liquid—that curious lurking something (as doubtless every objective from finally becomes to the subjective spirit), which means far more than its mere first sight, grand as that is—blending the real and ideal, and each made portion of the other. Hours, days, in my Long Island youth and early manhood, I haunted the shores of Rockaway or Coney island, or away east to the Hamptons or Montauk. Once, at the latter place, (by the old lighthouse, nothing but sea-tossings in sight in every direction as far as the eye could reach), I remember well, I felt that I must one day write a book, expressing this liquid, mystic theme. Afterward, I recollect, how it came to me that instead of any special lyrical or epical or literary attempt, the sea-shore should be an invisible *influence,* a pervading gauge and tally for me, in my composition. . . . There is a dream, a picture, that for years, at intervals, (sometimes quite long ones, but surely again, in time), has come noiselessly up before me, and I really believe, fiction as it is, has entered largely into my practical life—certainly into my writings, and shaped and colour'd them. It is nothing more or less than a stretch of interminable white-brown sand, hard and smooth and broad, with the ocean perpetually, grandly, rolling in upon it, with slow-measured sweep, with rustle and hiss and foam, and many a thump as of low bass drums. This scene, this picture, I say, has risen before me at times for years. Sometimes I wake at night and can hear and see it plainly.[4]

The interminable sea had not only an effect on his interminable sentences, but, operating on the universalising extensity of his fluid, emotional capacity, helped to make the physical universe for him a flux universe; and not the physical universe only, but the entire fabric raised by man's social, political, and ethical ideas. It cannot be doubted that to the profound influence which the sea exercised over his mind were due many of the forms and much of the significance of his mature *Weltanschauung*. On his fluid mind the flux world of his early experience left the most permanent impression; its phenomena suggested to him the imaginative moulds in which many of his mature ideas were cast, supplied the necessary imagery in which his mind afterwards bodied forth its fluid intuitions.

The Social Factor

In 1823, when he was about five years old, his parents removed to Brooklyn, where the next ten or eleven years of his life were spent. After completing his course at school, he worked for some years in the offices of lawyers, printers, and even chemists. In 1836/7 he was engaged in teaching on Long Island; and the fifteen years from 1840–1855 he spent chiefly in travelling through the states, absorbing the sights and studying the exuberant energies and ardent life with which the states were then teeming. His work during that period consisted chiefly in editing or contributing to newspapers in the principal cities, such as Brooklyn, New York, and New Orleans. Always a passionate lover of nature, and not devoid of that enthusiasm for what is big, which Americans have made peculiarly their own, he was profoundly impressed by the material resources and the immense area of his country. His mind which, as has been already pointed out, was of a very expansive nature, adapted itself to this vast natural environment; the parochial ideas of his Long Island childhood expanded into the cosmic ideas of his maturity.

In the meanwhile, another external factor had entered into the history of his growth. In the great American cities where he spent most of his time, he found not only the sea and nature, but also humanity—a human environment with its still more subtle suggestions and still more defiant appeal to that which was already rapidly taking shape in him—his personality. His travels through the various states, his sojourns in the great cities, and his profession as a journalist brought him in contact with varied types of individual and collective humanity. The hardy New England stock, to which he himself belonged, he knew most intimately. In the southern states he came in contact with a new type which, as his later work plainly indicates, had a very marked effect on him. The warm and ruddy South—the "magnet South" as he called it—appealed to the strong sensuous and imaginative element in his own nature, more perhaps than his native North, with its business energy and well-ordered progress could have done. It is probable that the South developed in him that instinct of lawlessness, that affinity to anarchism, and uncompromising individualism, which is so noticeable in his earlier work. Undoubtedly this "lawless" element was primordial in his personality, being but a phase of that fluid ideality, that disregard for constituted forms, which has been already noticed. But the South, which had not yet acquired the political training and the abiding legal and constitutional spirit which was ingrained in the North, turned this vague predisposition into a developed symptom.

On one point there is no doubt: wherever he found humanity, he found so much nourishment for his personality. The attractive forces that urged him towards his fellows were of tremendous strength and activity; and during this formative period, with its seething physical and intellectual energies, its friendships, its comradeships, its social yearnings and irresistible passions, which remained unrecorded but swelled the main account of his mature work, he laid the basis, in his own personal experience, of all those views of society, and the forces that sustain its health and life, which will be examined in due course. I quote only one of innumerable passages in which he relates the profound, almost inexplicable, effect which the phenomena of nature, and especially of society, made on his fluid personality and its growth:

Ah from a little child,
Thou knowest soul how to me all sounds became music,
My mother's voice in lullaby or hymn,
(The voice, O tender voices, memory's loving voices,
Last miracle of all, O dearest mother's, sister's, voices;)
The rain, the growing corn, the breeze among the long-leav'd corn,
The measur'd sea-surf beating on the sand,
The twittering bird, the hawk's sharp scream,
The wild-fowl's notes at night as flying low migrating north or
    south,
The psalm in the country church or mid the clustering trees, the
    open air camp-meeting,
The fiddler in the tavern, the glee, the long-strung sailor-song,
The lowing cattle, bleating sheep, the crowing cock at dawn.[5]

The Factor of Personality

But in the meantime his personality had not only socially
broadened; it had also deepened. Destiny had laid her hand on
him; at first very gently, but gradually with more force, till at
last he became conscious of her mighty presence. In the case of
the great personalities of the world this awakening to the still,
small voice—so small, yet so tremendous and irresistible—constitutes the supreme crisis in their lives. The dominating unconscious fuses with the consciousness mid fiery stress and strain;
the challenge of fate is accepted; the will forms a lasting alliance
with that necessity which it can neither understand nor resist;
and this alliance is usually accompanied by a readjustment of
the whole inner man. In the case of Whitman there was no such
crisis. His nature gradually deepened; duty did not oust impulse, but impulse gradually developed into something just as
potent and effective as duty. He gradually became aware that,
in the truest sense, his personality was unique; that the real
work he had to do was unique; that he could not think of those
prizes that his fellows were so ardently contending for. And in
his reminiscences, recorded in *Specimen Days,* we catch
glimpses of the steps by which this very slow transition was
effected. It is during the later part of this formative period that

we find him making prolonged solitary stays on the shores of Long Island, engaged in a deep study of the Bible and other masterpieces of antiquity, and in long spells of lonely meditation. Those who noted him during this period of his life afterwards said that he made the impression on them of being somewhat of a loafer, though not a bad sort; he seemed to take interest in nothing in particular. In fact, he was during this time outwardly lying fallow. A great work was being done, but no one noticed it. The great temple of his personality was being raised on the solid foundations of his nature and experience, but "neither hammer nor axe nor any tool of iron was heard while the house was in building".

The Absence of Crises

I have just referred to the absence, in Whitman's life, of a crisis at a period when it usually occurs in the case of other great personalities. With one more remark on this feature in Whitman's development I close the account of this period of his life. The absence of a crisis, of a violent transition or mental change, during this important period of his life, and indeed all periods of his life, is most significant both in regard to the light it throws on the nature of his personality and in regard to the far-reaching influence it exercised in moulding his opinions. A crisis indicates a want of harmony among the elements that constitute a man's total personality. There must be some original antagonism among the various elements coming to a head at some period of his life; or during the course of his growth different parts of him must have developed divergent interests and thus inevitably come to a collision. A harmonious nature knows no crisis. Goethe had no crisis; it may be confidently asserted that Shakespeare had none; it is certain that Whitman had none. This harmony of nature and growth showed itself, in the case of Whitman, in a remarkable continuity of development, in which it is almost impossible to discover a break or gap anywhere. This continuity of development prevented him from contracting any violent hatred or antipathy or prejudice;

it enabled him to "see life steadily and see it whole", according to his lights, without that bias to overrate here and under-rate there, which distinguishes the mind that has passed through crises. He never found occasion, for instance, to cast overboard the moral and religious ideas of his early youth; those ideas gradually expanded and merged into the vaster ethical and spiritual conceptions of his maturity. That largeness of outlook, that overflowing sympathy with all things human and divine, good and bad, which distinguished him through life, were in a great measure due to the even tenor of his mental growth. That proneness to assimilate distinctions and differences; that mental habit of sweeping together all things in one friendly aggregate (which have already been traced to his original mental constitution), which were fostered by the deep impression made on his fluid mind by the phenomena of the sea—were intensified by the even, unbroken, liquid, onward movement of his own supremely happy life. The absence of the element of strain and strenuousness, not only from his character and life, but also from his work, may be partly accounted for in this way. And this too is one of the reasons why the conception of duty scarcely occurs in his ethical code; why his entire conception of life is an outcome, not of moral stress and strain, but of that natural spontaneity in which his own personality was so rich.

4

Period of Naturalism
(1850-1861)

Leaves of Grass

IN 1855 *Leaves of Grass* appeared. Whitman had thought long about the form that his book had to take; he even made attempts in different styles. But he settled finally, and indeed inevitably, upon that professedly provisional form—half prose, half verse—which he used in all the later additions to *Leaves of Grass*.

He had in his composition that daring originality, that indifference to praise or blame, that largeness of conception, and above all that abundant vitality and faith which mark the pioneers or path-breakers of human progress. It was a daring book, remarkable in every respect. In it we find an American mechanic and newspaper writer grappling with the social, moral, and spiritual problems of the modern world with a candour, insight, and breadth of vision for which it would be hard to find a parallel. But the writer was greater than his book. As his brother said in answer to the question, what Whitman's family thought of *Leaves of Grass*—they thought it a great book, but him a greater man.

From the remarks made in Chapter 1, as to the unconscious elements in mental life, it follows that a man's views on his own work do not necessarily reflect its true character or significance. The personality is a natural phenomenon, only part of which is compassed by the eye of consciousness. It is only when the products of the personality are studied objectively as natural phenomena, and the evolution that connects them each with each is traced, that the nature of the personality and the true bearings of its work can be ascertained. And yet the conscious purpose, which a man has in view in his work and thought in life, is generally of the greatest importance in determining the character of that work. We therefore naturally ask what was Whitman's conscious purpose in writing *Leaves of Grass;* and he himself supplies the answer. His object was to describe the entire cosmos in its vast perspective as opened up by the scientific, philosophic, and social developments of the nineteenth century. But his survey is from a certain point of view, which forms its most important feature. His survey of the modern world does not in any way resemble the magnificent scheme of construction which Mr. Herbert Spencer has attempted in his synthetic philosophy. Not modern science, or philosophy, or society, forms his subject; his subject is the total impression produced on a wonderfully rich mind by the facts and phenomena of science, philosophy, and society. The vast range of modern thought and experience is coordinated from the point of view of a personality. This coordination was not quite successful until Whitman had caught clear sight of the idea of the whole, which will be described in Chapter 6; but the attempt to effect the coordination appears in his earliest mental efforts.

This is what Whitman himself said in after-years as to the inception and subject of *Leaves of Grass:*

After continued personal ambition and effort, as a young fellow, to enter with the rest into competition for the usual rewards, business, political, literary, etc.—to take part in the great *mêlée,* both for victory's prize itself and to do some good. After years of those aims and pursuits, I found myself remaining possess'd, at the age of thirty-one to thirty-three, with a special desire and conviction. Or rather, to be quite exact, a desire that had been flitting through my previous life, or hovering on the flanks, mostly indefinite hitherto, had steadily advanced to the front, defined itself, and finally dominated everything else. This was a feeling or ambition to articulate and faithfully express in literary or poetic form, and uncompromisingly, my own physical, emotional, moral, intellectual, and aesthetic Personality, in the midst of, and tallying, the momentous spirit and facts of its immediate days, and of current America— and to exploit that Personality, identified with place and date, in a far more candid and comprehensive sense than any hitherto poem or book.[1]

Subjectivity and Personality

Thus we see clearly what is the subject of *Leaves of Grass*. It is the personality of Whitman; it is a self-analysis, a self-portraiture. The main figure in the painting is Walt Whitman himself; while America, American civilisation, and nineteenth-century progress furnish the setting, the environment, the background to that figure.

What led Whitman to make his own personality the principal theme of *Leaves of Grass*? The question may seem purely speculative; but it is of great practical importance in that the answer will probably disclose to us the point of view from which Whitman regarded the phenomena of life and existence; in other words, will disclose to us the basis of Whitman's philosophy of life.

Let us revert for a moment to the analysis of Whitman's personality made in Chapter 2. It was there shown that the basic quality of his mind was ideality, emotionality, spirituality; in short, what was there called the "flux" quality. It was then shown how this quality was nourished into strength by the phenomena of the sea, and into maturity by his experience of the extremely mobile and fluid movements of American society and life. His attraction both towards the sea and large masses of men shows that such phenomena supplied the food after which his mind was hungering. Thus was developed in him the "flux" personality; and as man ultimately can see in the mirror of the objective world nothing but his own image, the universe became for him a "flux" universe. The statical view of the world and society was thus alien to his very nature. To him there was nothing stationary or even stable in the whole universe. Everything was in eternal flux and progress, surging from a beginning that lies beyond the thought of man to an end that can never be reached. To the wise and thoughtful there has always been certainty or permanence somewhere. To some, the idea of God supplies such a point of rest; to others, the absolute in philosophy, or the authority of the wise, or of the sovereign or state, or the dictates of duty, furnish such resting-points, centres of certainty, anchors of safety within the eternal float of illimitable circumstance. But to Whitman, who was a Heraclitan evolutionist by nature, there was, before he fully realised the idea of the whole, no such point of certainty or permanence in the "great unrest" of which he was a part. Seven years before Herbert Spencer published his *First Principles,* four years before Darwin's *Origin of Species* appeared, Whitman gave, in the first edition of *Leaves of Grass,* the following matchless account of human evolution:

I am an acme of things accomplish'd, and I an encloser of things
    to be.
My feet strike an apex of the apices of the stairs,
On every step bunches of ages, and larger bunches between the
    steps,
All below duly travel'd, and still I mount and mount.

Rise after rise bow the phantoms behind me,
Afar down I see the huge first Nothing, I know I was even there,
I waited unseen and always, and slept through the lethargic mist,
And took my time, and took no hurt from the fetid carbon.

Long I was hugg'd close—long and long.

Immense have been the preparations for me,
Faithful and friendly the arms that have help'd me.

Cycles ferried my cradle, rowing and rowing like cheerful boatmen,
For room to me stars kept aside in their own rings,
They sent influences to look after what was to hold me.

Before I was born out of my mother generations guided me,
My embryo has never been torpid, nothing could overlay it.

For it the nebula cohered to an orb,
The long slow strata piled to rest it on,
Vast vegetables gave it sustenance,
Monstrous sauroids transported it in their mouths and deposited
    it with care.

All forces have been steadily employ'd to complete and delight me,
Now on this spot I stand with my robust soul.[2]

The last line must not be taken to mean that at last a fixed
point has been reached in the forward motion; for a little later
on in the same poem he indicates that he, too, is a part of that
motion:

I tramp a perpetual journey, (come listen all!)
My signs are a rain-proof coat, good shoes, and a staff cut from
    the woods,
No friend of mine takes his ease in my chair,
I have no chair, no church, no philosophy,
I lead no man to a dinner-table, library, exchange,
But each man and each woman of you I lead upon
    a knoll,
My left hand hooking you round the waist,
My right hand pointing to landscapes of continents
    and the public road.[3]

And the endless evolution will proceed till what is now called
man will mark but a link in the perfected chain which will
join the primordial Nothing to the ultimate All.

My rendezvous is appointed, it is certain,
The Lord will be there and wait till I come on perfect terms,
The great Camerado, the lover true for whom I pine will be there.[4]

Thus Whitman's fluid mind dissolved all the fixed ideas of
former thought. The physical universe, man, society, morality,
religion, were for him but sections of the eternal, universal unrest and uncertainty.

Now, if he wished to contribute something towards the forces
of progress, he had to fix his attention somewhere. He had to
take up some commanding position in the biodynamic immen-

sity from which to survey and coordinate the phenomena of human life. What wonder that that position was his own personality? Personality was his distinguishing attribute and possession. In every human being it is the element of destiny which ultimately determines and controls the activities of all the other forces of his nature. Why not describe that personality—its inner mysteries; its revelation in, and attitude towards, the world of sense and society? Here at any rate appears, if not a fixed and unchangeable, then a constant element, existing and operating wherever man is found. Here a master's hand may yet do a master's work. Thus Whitman was inevitably led, both by his inner promptings and the point of view from which he regarded the cosmos, to take personality as his subject.

If this explanation should seem wanting in clearness, the matter may be otherwise put as follows. If modern philosophy has, in its vain endeavours to formulate some true and consistent scheme of the universe, anywhere stumbled upon a fundamental truth, it is this: that all knowledge is relative; and that the startingpoint for arriving at any correct conclusions is not some far-off spot in the continent of being, but man himself —the individual observer or thinker himself. A man may be in terrible doubt about his conclusions, either as to the existence or the characteristics of the objective world. He has no such doubts about his own sensations, wishes, thoughts. Whether the objective world be a mere subjective illusion or not, a sane man is at any rate very certain about his own wants and feelings, and the part played by his surroundings (whatever they may be in themselves) in satisfying or stimulating these. Thus in philosophy man inevitably becomes the centre of the universe; as no one can transcend the data of his own personality, everyone becomes a standard by which he consciously or otherwise judges the whole universe. Now Whitman, partly by a process of reasoning, of which indications are scattered through his prose work, but chiefly by the unconscious operation of the forces of his personality, has made this cardinal point of philosophy the centre of his cosmic survey in *Leaves of Grass;* has made the personality, chiefly of himself, its great theme, its centre of reference, so to speak, round which all the detail is grouped. It was his belief that the primordial personality was the supreme in every individual; that it had not to be subjected to anyone or anything external, however high or sacred; that there was no absolute authority over it anywhere existent, either in the dictates of duty or the commands of the state or of the majority; that all these, and the external world generally, were only competent to supply the necessary material in the evolution and "projection of the soul on its lone way". Without ever maintaining the absurd opinion that the world was made for man, he yet held that the world, or all those forces that operate outside of the personality, were there, not to crush or overwhelm or paralyse the individual, but to help and sustain him along the path of destiny.

It must not be rashly inferred from these remarks that Whitman was what is now called an individualist. There is a great difference between the philosophy of personalism and that of individualism.

It will be noticed that, in the quotation made at the end of the preceding section, Whitman confesses that the subject of *Leaves of Grass* is not so much personality in general as his special personality. To some this choice of a subject has proved an insuperable stumbling-block to a due appreciation of *Leaves of Grass*. To them Whitman appears to have been egged on by inordinate and uncontrollable vanity towards a nauseous, incessant practice of self-revelation. And probably many readers, accustomed to look more for the little self-repressions, courtesies, and polite urbanities under which literary self-conceit often conceals itself than for the vital things of thought and life, bluntly and straightforwardly expressed, have been shocked and repelled by the constant use of the first personal pronoun by this blatant American pamphleteer and high-falutin' eulogist of the universe and America. Fancy a so-called poet without silk handkerchiefs and white gloves; who, moreover, has the audacity to write his longest and not least successful poem on himself! It is enough to strike dumb all the cultured and altruistic coteries of Philistia.

The serious student, however, does not need to read very far in *Leaves of Grass* before he discovers that his use of the first personal pronoun has a peculiar significance. *The egoism of Whitman is objective.* He does not celebrate or glory in those qualities which differentiate him from his fellows, but in those which he possesses in common with them. What he celebrates in himself are just those qualities that make him one of the "divine average" for whom he sings.

This method of treating the individual—whatever it may be —not in itself or for itself, but as a type, is a familiar one with Whitman, and we shall meet it again and again in the course of this inquiry. Indeed, it is the method which one would naturally expect from one who took the standpoint sketched above. It also follows directly from the fundamental characteristics of his personality; for while the fluid, ideal side of his mind tends to show itself in treating of the general, of the universal, as distinguished from the particular, his realistic bent, on the other hand, keeps him from mere abstractions and compels him to utilise the individual in the illustration of the general or universal. Further reference to this will be made later on. It is sufficient to note here, as one of Whitman's distinctive methods, his refusal to treat the individual—be it person or thing or quality or thought or emotion—merely in itself. His method may be described as the concrete-general, or the typical-general. His real subject is the general, but not the abstract general. He treats of the general only by means of the concrete instance or typical particular. If he writes about himself—his thoughts, feelings, hopes, joys, aspirations—his object is to describe these states of mind as they exist more or less in all persons. If he commends himself for the possession of certain qualities, he does so in order to commend or induce or strengthen the same qualities in others. The "Song of Myself", for instance, opens thus:

> I celebrate myself, and sing myself,
> And what I assume you shall assume,
> For every atom belonging to one as good belongs to you.[5]

The Individual Personality

Having thus seen that Whitman's subject is personality, especially as illustrated by the manifestations of his own, it remains still to inquire in what special respects he treats of the personality; what attributes he assigns to it, and what functions in the evolution, not only of the individual life, but also of the social organism.

The human individual can be looked upon in two very different aspects: either as an individual entity, or as a member of society; either as an end in himself, or as a subordinate though very significant unit in the organic whole of human society. Even in the former aspect—even when viewed merely as an individual—the effect on the personality of the influences due to society must be profound, and to that extent the distinction is not a real one, theoretically. But it does practically make a great difference whether we look upon the individual as an individual, influenced indeed by social forces around him, but only influenced; or whether we regard him as more properly a mere function in the activities of the social organism. In the one case we look upon man as a social *individual;* in the other, as a *social* individual. Now Whitman's work consists of a very profound treatment of the personality in both these respects—in its individual and its social aspects. *Leaves of Grass* opens with these lines:

> One's-Self I sing, a simple separate person,
> Yet utter the word Democratic, the word En-Masse.[6]

This is his own statement of the subject and scope of his work. And looking upon that work as the product of an organically developing personality, and stating the result in terms of the distinction above drawn, we may say that his early work had reference chiefly to the personality in its individual and obvious social aspects; that his grasp of the more profound social aspects of the personality deepened as his experience and thoughtfulness increased; while in the final portions of his work we notice a tendency to identify the individual with the spiritual destinies of the race; and the personality, raised to a higher emotional and spiritual capacity by the social forces which have played through the individual life, reaches its last and highest consummation.

What attributes does Whitman assign to the individual personality, and how does he link it to the society in which alone it reaches its highest manifestations? Here the "form" of Whitman's personality will once more prove helpful. To the flux element in his personality, coalescing with certain cognate elements in his experience, have been traced his disregard for established forms and results, and his constant regard of the forces which have produced those results. And it has been noted that, but for the operation of another factor in his personality, this mode of thinking and looking at the world might have led him to anarchism. And indeed anarchism (in the higher sense of the term) is the most persistent note in his paean to the individual. His earlier work especially shows, more than that of any other literary thinker, the intimate causal relation, the interchangeability of anarchism and certain phases of individualism. It may be added here that there is nothing offensive or permanently dangerous in this anarchism. It is only the conception of the sway of those divine-brute energies whose silent workings are seen, not only in the highest religious ideas of our race, but also in the world-transforming enthusiasm of its greatest leaders. There is something greater than the creation—the creator; there are things greater than order and stability—the forces whose progressive activities underlie order and stability; there are things more valuable than the most highly treasured institutions of society—the human heart and head which, consciously or unconsciously, make and unmake those institutions. This is the conception of the higher anarchism which pervades Whitman's treatment of the individual personality.

I heard it was charged against me that I sought to destroy institutions,
But really I am neither for nor against institutions,

(What indeed have I in common with them? Or what with the
    destruction of them?)
Only I will establish in the Mannahatta, and in every city of these
    States inland and seaboard,
And in the fields and woods, and above every keel little or large
    that dents the water,
Without edifice or rules or trustees or any argument,
The institution of the dear love of comrades.[7]

The final turn of this passage shows that it really belongs to
another department of Whitman's work; it is in fact taken from
"Calamus". The poem that expounds at greatest length and
in the most uncompromising outspokenness the doctrine of the
individual personality, of the "simple separate Person", is
"Song of Myself", which appeared in the first edition of *Leaves
of Grass*. Some have said that it contains really everything of
importance in *Leaves of Grass*. But if the view of Whitman's
development which is expounded in this book be correct, the
"Song of Myself" supplies but the initial words of Whitman's
message to the world. It is but the first chapter in that long
history of personal evolution which is recorded in *Leaves of
Grass*. It describes, perhaps with greater force and truth than
any other poem in all literature, the separate individual, divine
in his own right, stripped of all social clothes, sansculottic,
anarchistic, revolutionary, bent on progress and self-realisation
at all hazards, even at the expense of all that the social sentiments hallow and endear. It may therefore be well to look a
little more closely at this poem, as it undoubtedly throws a
great light on Whitman's individual personality and, by im-
plication, on individuality in general.

Two passages in "Song of Myself" are fundamental. The first
mentions the inscrutable creative impulse of the world-energy,
which forms the root of progress:

        Urge and urge and urge,
        Always the procreant urge of the world.[8]

The second passage notes the presence of this cosmic impulse
in the basic constitution of the individual.

There is that in me—I do not know what it is—but I know it is
in me.

. . . .

I do not know it—it is without name—it is a word unsaid,
It is not in any dictionary, utterance, symbol.[9]

Here, then, the taproot of the individuality is reached. Here we
are abruptly brought face to face with that greatest mystery in
the universe—a little centre of life-force vitalising and organis-
ing dull, inert matter. It is this central force, urging and propelling a certain quantity of accrementitious matter, that constitutes the basis of the personality in every man, the portion
of destiny operating in and through him, working as his heart
beats—uncontrolled by will or consciousness—and unfolding,
like all other organic forces, its inner character and capabilities
in the history of the individual life.

Now as soon as this central force of the individual personality begins to work within the sphere of organised society, it becomes, to a certain extent, subject to the social forces. But so
long and so far as it is considered by itself, untrammelled by
the superior sway of the social forces, it is supreme. Now what
are some of the characteristics of Whitman's individual personality when supposed to be in this state of nature and apart
from the controlling play of the social forces?

In the first place, as we have already seen, Whitman's individual personality is anarchistic, disdains existing forms, and
indeed utilises those forms only so far as they contribute towards its sustenance and progress. Says he:

I am for those that have never been master'd,
For men and women whose tempers have never been master'd,
For those whom laws, theories, conventions, can never master.[10]

And again, in another poem:

As I lay with my head in your lap camerado,
The confession I made I resume, what I said to you and the open
air I resume,
I know I am restless and make others so,
I know my words are weapons full of danger, full of death,

For I confront peace, security, and all the settled laws, to unsettle
  them,
I am more resolute because all have denied me than I could ever
  have been had all accepted me,
I heed not and have never heeded either experience, cautions,
  majority, nor ridicule,
And the threat of what is call'd hell is little or nothing to me,
And the lure of what is call'd heaven is little or nothing to me;
Dear camerado! I confess I have urged you onward with me, and
  still urge you, without the least idea what is our destination,
Or whether we shall be victorious, or utterly quell'd and defeated.[11]

Secondly, his individual personality favours equality; it ex-
tends to one and all the right it claims for itself—to exist, to
grow, to live according to its inner primordial laws. And it may
be here noted that not only in "Song of Myself", but all
through Whitman's work, we hear this voice of passionate
pleading for equality; the equal right of every one, irrespective
of race or sex, to bring out the talent which destiny has wrapped
up in the folds of his nature. In "Song of Myself", especially,
this pleading has a note of fierceness, of self-assertive energy,
because there the individual speaks for himself and in his own
right.

Thirdly, Whitman's individuality is marked by a passion for
progress—this being merely the active side of his emotional
fluidity. It is perhaps doubtful whether any other poet has ever
sung in equally impressive language and with equal passion
the great cause of progress. In his mind progress was identified
not only with the self-realisation and happiness of the individual, but also with the future of his own America and the
human race. For America it was no longer possible to direct
her turbulent energies into the channel of foreign warfare.
Her ideal was to be peace, industry, commerce, and the higher
civilisation which is based on this material one. The terrible
forces, both for good and evil, stored up in her had to find an
outlet somewhere, and that outlet was to be progress along the
great paths of civilisation. But for such progress her energies
must be spent in self-destruction and result in the self-exhaus-

tion which seems to characterise the oriental world. And for the individual, too, there is true happiness only in honest toil, in unremitting effort. Hence his felicitous summing-up of the so-called Gospel of Work:

> (Ah little recks the laborer,
> How near his work is holding him to God,
> The loving Laborer through space and time.)[12]

Hence, too, his impressive warning to states and men:

> Fear grace, elegance, civilization, delicatesse,
> Fear the mellow sweet, the sucking of honey-juice,
> Beware the advancing mortal ripening of Nature,
> Beware what precedes the decay of the ruggedness of states
>   and men.[13]

And hence, too, the persistence with which he recurs to the song of the cause of progress, of forward striving, of ceaseless effort. Indeed, from this point of view *Leaves of Grass* may be considered a commentary on those lines in which Goethe sums up the moral and philosophy of his *Faust*:

> *Wer immer strebend sich bemüht,*
> *Den können wir erlösen.*[14]

On account of its growing passion and hope, its metrical swing, and the simplicity of its rhythms, "Pioneers, O Pioneers" is perhaps the best-known poem of Whitman; and it is a song of progress. But a poem of far deeper meaning on the same subject is "Song of the Open Road". The whole piece is deserving of careful study; a few stanzas may here be quoted, in which Whitman draws a picture of the great army of progress.

Allons! after the great Companions, and to belong to them!
They too are on the road—they are the swift and majestic men—
    they are the greatest women,
Enjoyers of calms of seas and storms of seas,
Sailors of many a ship, walkers of many a mile of land,
Habitués of many distant countries, habitués of far-distant dwellings,
Trusters of men and women, observers of cities, solitary toilers,

. . . .

71

Fourth-steppers from the latent unrealised baby-days,
Journeyers gayly with their own youth, journeyers with their bearded
    and well-grain'd manhood,
Journeyers with their womanhood, ample, unsurpass'd, content,
Journeyers with their sublime old age of manhood or womanhood,
Old age, calm, expanded, broad with the haughty breadth of the
    universe,
Old age, flowing free with the delicious near-by freedom of death.

Allons! to that which is endless as it was beginningless,
To undergo much, tramps of days, rests of nights,
. . . .
To see no possession but you may possess it, enjoying all without
    labor or purchase, abstracting the feast yet not abstracting
    one particle of it.
. . . .
To gather the minds of men out of their brains as you encounter
    them, to gather the love out of their hearts,
To take your lovers on the road with you, for all that you leave
    them behind you,
To know the universe itself as a road, as many roads, as roads for
    travelling souls.
. . . .
Of the progress of the souls of men and women along the grand
    roads of the universe, all other progress is the needed emblem
    and sustenance.

Forever alive, forever forward,
Stately solemn, sad, withdrawn, baffled, mad, turbulent, feeble,
    dissatisfied,
Desperate, proud, fond, sick, accepted by men, rejected by men,
They go! they go! I know that they go, but I know not where they
    go,
But I know that they go toward the best—toward something great.[15]

As we gaze at the pageantry of progress here painted, as we
listen to the song of progress here sung with such passion, we
become aware that the progress of the individual or the race
is not celebrated for its own sake merely, but also because it is,
in the poet's mind, part of and identified with the tides and

pulsations of that hidden life that flows eternally through all
things. That this is so, that human progress is in Whitman's
mind a manifestation of the divine life of the whole, appears
from the pregnant lines in "Faces":

> The Lord advances, and yet advances,
> Always the shadow in front, always the reach'd hand
>   bringing up the laggards.[16]

"Song of the Open Road" ends with the following beautiful
lines, which show the intensity of the personal element in
Leaves of Grass:

> Camerado, I give you my hand!
> I give you my love more precious than money,
> I give you myself before preaching or law;
> Will you give me yourself? Will you come travel with me?
> Shall we stick by each other as long as we live? [17]

The same strain of exultant joy at the contemplation of progress, of remonstrance and exhortation to others to dedicate
themselves to progress, is heard all through Whitman's poems
till the very end. And notwithstanding his sanity and common
sense, he never hesitated to celebrate, in the interests of progress, those dreamers and rapt enthusiasts whose devotion and
ideas mark, in one degree or another, the turning-points along
the path of progress.

In the fourth place, as an individual Whitman refuses to
recognise those moral, social, and religious distinctions which
have their origin and discharge their functions more properly
in organised society. The outcast is recognised and treated with
as much deference as the social favourite or immaculate; the
good are not preferred to the bad, the strong to the weak, the
healthy to the sick. Over them all, with equal benignance and
beneficence the sunshine of the poet's sympathy and fellow-feeling falls. He is not in any sense a respecter of persons. Thus he
says in "Song of Myself":

> I speak the pass-word primeval, I give the sign of democracy,
> By God! I will accept nothing which all cannot have their
>   counter-part of on the same terms,

Through me many long dumb voices,
Voices of the interminable generations of prisoners and slaves,
Voices of the diseas'd and despairing and of thieves and dwarfs,
Voices of cycles of preparation and accretion,

. . . .

And of the rights of them the others are down upon,
Of the deform'd, trivial, flat, foolish, despised,
Fog in the air, beetles rolling balls of dung.[18]

This sympathy for those that have failed, for the oppressed and weak and lost, finds constant expression in *Leaves of Grass,* and was certainly one of the most deeply felt emotions in his wonderfully rich nature. Thus, in a poem written in after-life, "From Noon to Starry Night", we find the following:

I see the enslaved, the overthrown, the hurt, the opprest of the
   whole earth,
I see the measureless shame and humiliation of my race, it
   becomes all mine,
Mine too the revenges of humanity, the wrongs of ages, baffled
   feuds and hatreds;
Utter defeat upon me weighs—all lost—the foe victorious,
(Yet 'mid the ruins Pride colossal stands unshaken to the last,
Endurance, resolution to the last.) [19]

Not only do these words possess a deep pathos by the light of Whitman's self-sacrificing devotion to hospital work, but they are also remarkable—in their expression of invincible and undying devotion to and fellow-feeling for the wreckage of humanity—as coming from the poet of athletes, of physical strength and perfection.

However admirable all will find this love and sympathy for the degraded and lost, what must be said of Whitman's apparent wiping away of the distinctions between virtue and vice, right and wrong, and his refusal—in so many parts of his work —to recognise the ordinary moral distinctions? It is undoubted that this has repelled many readers from *Leaves of Grass.* It is equally undoubted that no sane man—and certainly not Walt Whitman—would wish to see the disappearance from society of these moral ideas which, as they are the most powerful and necessary bonds of social existence and progress, it has also cost and still is costing the race most time and suffering to acquire and maintain. The moral heritage of humanity is only less precious and dearly bought than its spiritual heritage; and no man ought lightly to presume that he can touch it with impunity. What, then, must be said of Whitman's ignoring of moral distinctions? Thus he says in "Song of Myself":

I am not the poet of goodness only, I do not decline to be the
    poet of wickedness also.

What blurt is this about virtue and about vice?
Evil propels me and reform of evil propels me, I stand indifferent,
My gait is no fault-finder's or rejecter's gait,
I moisten the roots of all that has grown.[20]

And again, in "Starting from Paumanok":

Omnes! Omnes! let others ignore what they may,
I make the poem of evil also, I commemorate that part also,
I am myself just as much evil as good, and my nation is—
    and I say there is in fact no evil,
(Or if there is I say it is just as important to you, to the land
    or to me, as any thing else.) [21]

These passages state Whitman's position with tolerable accuracy. Many possible inferences from his free language must be discounted on the ground of its poetic exaggeration. And so far as his mergence of moral ideas is seriously intended, it is at least intelligible from his point of view. For, as he refused to recognise any inherent evil in what society accounted wrong, his advocacy of equality and his equal recognition of all operative forces in the universe compel him to accord to those ideas that society ostracises an equal status with those she favours; he is obliged to treat outcast ideas with the same tolerant generosity as outcast persons. And this position he accepts most cheerfully. He fails to see how harm can come from such outcast ideas, provided they be kept within their due limits by the equal sway of the socially favoured ideas.

The above passages also show that Whitman relies on evil as

one of the causes that make for progress. Is it not the case that our natural conservatism or inertia of disposition makes us shrink but too readily from all efforts that make for progress? And does the belief that we already possess something worth having not strengthen in us the disinclination to strive for something better still? And is the good not in this sense the constant and inevitable enemy of the better? Truly, if the better had not usually the bad for an ally, it would never make any headway against the good, entrenched behind the *status quo!* Now Whitman, knowing all this, and being in the deepest sense a revolutionary, a reformer who had a passion for progress, and being withal perfectly honest and fair-minded, was obliged to celebrate evil, too, as one of the most potent factors in progress.

On a closer scrutiny, however, it becomes evident that there is a more fundamental difference between the conventional standpoint and that taken by Whitman. As he habitually looked through the forms and shows of things to the underlying operative forces and energies, he inevitably came to neglect the empirical rules which society has drawn up for her own safety, and he regarded more the dominant impulse of life surging beneath these rules. In other words he was, like Goethe, more a profound student of life than a votary of ethics. The qualities that make for strength and health, for the fullest, healthiest, richest life, concern him more than those which fall within the province of the ethical philosopher or moralist. And further: we have seen already that Whitman adopted, in accordance with the constitutional bent of his mind, the standpoint of subjective relativity as the centre of reference, not only of his philosophy, but also in his poetic method. A thing, action, quality, was to him not good or bad in itself, but only in so far as it did or did not contribute towards the efficiency and realisation of the individual or society. As he had adopted this subjective point of view, and looked at moral phenomena from the standpoint of the person, he consistently refused to recognise so-called objective standards of moral distinction outside the individual consciousness. In personality he recognised, and recognised rightly, the highest manifestation of life in this world. The personality

—that life which underlies the head and heart and soul of man —indicates the highest watermark in that rising wave of evolution which has been rolling forward from the beginning. What is the right, the good? Does it exist? Is it a reality at all in itself? Is it not rather a broken fragment of the whole—of the personality? Does the right not constitute merely one of the rays into which the white light of the personality can be resolved? The person is the mysterious, highest constructive effort of nature; and as such he is greater and higher than the right, or the good, or the beautiful, which are but abstract fragments of the concrete whole. Why, then, should the person subordinate the wholesome activities of his nature to intangible and incogniscible abstractions? Is this subjection of man to abstract ideas not an effect of that pernicious habit of thinkers—already referred to in Chapter 2—of mistaking the abstract for the concrete? The path of progress has up to the present been the path not of abstractions, but of reality; of concrete realisation; of slow, painful groping towards *esse* of that which before was only *posse*. The process is not likely to be reversed now. The individual may and ought to try more and more to incorporate into his personality, to realise more and more in his life, those intuitions of the right, the good, the beautiful, of which he is in one degree or another conscious. But let him not substitute for the evolution of his full personality the possibly thwarting and cramping domination of abstract moral ideas. Let these ideas help and suggest; let them not rule or dominate.

The empirical rules of morality are no doubt most valuable and estimable things; but why should they straight-jacket and imprison the life within? Why should, in the hierarchy of our moral constitution, the policeman be placed above the statesman? The rough and ready distinctions of conventional morality are valueless in the case of a spiritual mind like Whitman's, and must in any case vanish before the imperious necessities of personal evolution.

Ascending from the empirical prescriptions for a moral life, we come to that high notion of abstract "right" which dominates, so far as I know, all modern systems of ethical philosophy

—the coign of vantage whence the whole field of moral phe-nomena is surveyed and examined. Has the idea of "right" the authority to dominate our moral philosophy when its contents and even nature are so notoriously vague and uncertain as to have formed a matter of dispute among all thinkers in all ages? Far be it from me to belittle this noble and precious intuition of the soul, groping instinctively towards the light that shines beyond the borders of present reality. But it seems to me that, after all, the true function of the idea of right is not to form a Procrustes bed on which the fair forms of practical evolution are maimed and tortured, but to brace the but-too-often flaccid moral physique of the personality, to be the tonic of our con-science in its action in practical life. Thus the right is really but a function of the personality; not a standard *ab extra* for determining the ethical or other value of the personality.[22]

I hope that this is not an incorrect representation of the basis of Whitman's ethical ideas during this period of naturalism. It will be shown later on how in this, as in all other departments of his mental activity, his work shows indisputable evidence of development, of progress beyond this somewhat naturalistic standpoint. His biological point of view remained the same, though the spiritualisation of his mind influenced his ethical vision.

The above statements may sound like mere truisms, and yet it is probable that a frank recognition and application of them will necessitate extensive changes of ethical philosophy. When the attempt to construct abstract standards of ethical conduct—that *damnosa haereditas* of mediaeval scholasticism—is seen to be wrong; when the personality is seen to be the only true standard; when it is seen and admitted that, in the interests of all true progress, the normal person must, within the limits and restraints of the social environment be, for better or for worse, a law unto himself—it seems that the vast superstruc-ture of Western ethical speculation is shaken to its very founda-tions. It is noteworthy that the organic changes introduced by Christianity into Western religion were due largely to the sub-stitution of a supreme personality for the abstractions and fictions that had gone before. And it is impossible to study carefully the lives and opinions of some of the greatest personalities that Western civilisation has produced (Goethe, for instance) and not to conclude that they have thrown down a gauntlet to abstract moralists, which the latter have never yet taken up. *Leaves of Grass,* in particular, forms such a challenge to philosophy, which I hope will some day be accepted.

While this passion for progress and equality, this averseness to recognise ordinary moral distinctions, are products of the flux tendency in Whitman's mind, another quality that must now be referred to is directly traceable to his realism. It is difficult to find a term which will include all the phases of this quality. If the word "sanity" is used in both a physical and mental sense, it will probably do better than any other. This sanity, then, this inward harmony and balance of mind, this external attraction to all that is healthy and real, this devotion to nature, to outdoor life and pursuits, to sunshine and open air, constitutes another characteristic of Whitman's mind.

One phase of this sanity is the curious calmness of imperturbability which was as characteristic of the man Whitman as it was of his work. It was because of the absence in him of all feverish excitements that he could look with such invincible calmness on the painfully slow unfolding of truth in this world.

> All truths wait in all things,
> They neither hasten their own delivery nor resist it,
> They do not need the obstetric forceps of the surgeon,
> The insignificant is as big to me as any.[23]

Whitman's love for and devotion to outside nature and the ordinary physical facts is attested not only by the general spirit of his writings, but in particular by a number of his larger poems (such as "A Song of Occupations", "Song of the Broad-Axe", "Song of the Redwood-Tree", etc.). It is in this love of and continual contact with external nature that Whitman finds one cure for the physical and moral ills of a society largely engaged in factories, workshops, offices, and in urban occupations generally. "Perhaps indeed", he says, "the efforts of the true poets, founders, religions, literatures, all ages, have been, and ever will be, our times and times to come, essentially the same —to bring people back from their persistent strayings and sickly abstractions to the costless, average, divine, original concrete".[24]

The function of literature in inculcating the lessons of practical contact with external nature is thus expressed in "Democratic Vistas":

Present literature, while magnificently fulfilling certain popular demands, with plenteous knowledge and verbal smartness, is profoundly sophisticated, insane, and its very joy is morbid. It needs to tally and express Nature, and the spirit of Nature, and to know and obey the standards. I say the question of Nature, largely consider'd, involves the questions of the aesthetic, the emotional, and the religious—and involves happiness. A fitly born and bred race, growing up in right conditions of out-door as much as in-door harmony, activity and development, would probably, from and in those conditions, find it enough merely *to live*—and would, in their relations to the sky, air, water, trees, etc., and to the countless common shows, and in the fact of life itself, discover and achieve happiness—with Being suffused night and day by wholesome extasy, surpassing all the pleasures that wealth, amusement and even gratified intellect, erudition, or the sense of art, can give.[25]

The precept of harmony with nature and the concrete real, which Whitman makes for the physical and moral well-being of urbanised society, he applied consistently—some say with disastrous results to his poetic reputation—in his own poetic practice. In art and literature he sedulously avoided whatever seemed to him to deflect from that sanity and naturalness which he prized above all things. His grand test for poetry was its correspondence with facts—the facts of external nature; the facts of internal human nature in its healthy and normal activities. Thus at one stroke he severed all possible connection with the regular machinery of popular poetry, with the sentimental, the morbid, the superfine workmanship, the bloom of decay which sleeps with such pensive beauty over outworn ideas and institutions in most contemporary poetry. He himself states with perfect lucidity the position he had taken up from the very start: "I wanted, and still want for poetry, the clear sun shining, and fresh air blowing—the strength and power of health, not of delirium, even amid the stormiest passions—with always the background of the eternal moralities".[26] No wonder that for him the following were among the great topics of poetry:

Divine instinct, breadth of vision, the law of reason, health, rudeness
    of body, withdrawnness,
Gayety, sun-tan, air-sweetness, such are some of the words of poems.[27]

This passion for sanity, this attraction to all that is healthy and normal in the universe, combined with his internal balance and harmony of mind, ultimately found expression in the fundamental belief and assumption of his later writings: the moral sanity and unity of the whole cosmos, and the great end of life and thought as being the realisation of that sanity and harmony in the individual life. That belief will be examined in Chapter 6.

We come now to the last aspect of Whitman's individual personality to which reference will be made. This is its religious aspect.

The mention of this subject in this connection raises several important preliminary questions. First: Is religion more a product of personal than of social evolution? Second: Does the treatment of the subject of religion properly fall within this period of naturalism? Third: What is meant by the term "religion"?

The first question—whether religion is to be more properly considered a product of the individual development—will be answered generally in Chapter 7. But the undoubted fact, that the sentiments and aspirations that cluster around the complex conceptions of religion are, in their highest and purest forms, intuitions and experiences of the individual soul, however much they may be nourished from the social sentiments, seems to make this the most logical connection in which to start a discussion of this important aspect of Whitman's development and work.

The answer to the second question depends purely on evidence; and the evidence that even in this period of naturalism Whitman was deeply influenced by a religious cast of thought and a religious purpose will soon be adduced. And, if we bear in mind that naturalism does not in this connection bear the stigma which has generally been fixed on the term by different schools of religious and philosophic thought, there is nothing strange in this association of naturalism and religion. When I say that, during this period of his development Whitman's view of man's nature was largely naturalistic, phenomenal, animal, this does not in any way imply that his view was immoral. For the human animal, so long as it is natural and normal in its activities, is clean and sweet—qualities which have always been considered akin to godliness. A rich and thoughtful nature may start with a biological, physical, animal view of man; and yet that view may have in it the germs of, and ultimately attain to, the highest and purest spirituality—as was the case with Whitman.

To the third question—what religion is—it is impossible to return any answer. In Chapters 6 and 7 I shall attempt to give an explanation of the principal religious ideas and their sources, as they occur in Whitman's writings. But to define religion is clearly impossible. For what is a definition but a statement of a name or thing in more generally recognised terms—a reduction of a complex function to simpler factors and elements? But as religion embraces the last and highest experiences of the human personality, it clearly involves elements which do not exist in the lower ranges of experience; and the reduction of religion to, or its expression in terms of, lower and simpler ideas, is apparently impossible. Just as it is impossible to express the phenomena of life in terms of force and energy; just as it is impossible to state the phenomena of thought completely in terms of the similar biological conceptions, so it seems impossible completely to reduce religion to more generally recognised forms of experience. I can only attempt to show that a general religious purpose underlay *Leaves of Grass* from the very start, and to state some of the more obvious features of that religious purpose, leaving the fuller development of the topic for later chapters.

That within the purview and for the purpose of that system of practical philosophy, and morality, and sociology which Whitman originally intended to inaugurate in *Leaves of Grass*, religion is a subject of fundamental—of overshadowing—importance, appears again and again from his writings. Take the following passage, written in 1872:

When I commenced, years ago, elaborating the plan of my poems, and continued turning over that plan, and shifting it in my mind through many years, (from the age of twenty-eight to thirty-five,) experimenting much, and writing and abandoning much, one deep purpose underlay the others, and has underlain it and its execution ever since—and that has been the religious purpose. Not of course to exhibit itself in the old ways, as in writing hymns or psalms with an eye to the church-pew, or to express conventional pietism, or the sickly yearnings of devotees, but in new ways, and aiming at the widest sub-bases and inclusions of humanity, and tallying the fresh air of sea and land.[28]

Or take, again, the following from "Starting from Paumanok", an important poem which appeared in 1856:

The soul,
Forever and forever—longer than soil is brown and solid—longer
    than water ebbs and flows.

Know you, solely to drop in the earth the germs of a greater
    religion,
The following chants each for its kind I sing.

Each is not for its own sake,
I say the whole earth and all the stars in the sky are for
    religion's sake,
I say no man has ever yet been half devout enough,
None has ever yet adored or worship'd half enough,

*None has begun to think how divine he himself is, and how
certain the future is.*

I say that the real and permanent grandeur of these States
    must be their religion,
Otherwise there is no real and permanent grandeur;
(Nor character nor life worthy the name without religion,
    Nor land nor man nor woman without religion.) [29]

From the line I have italicised in this quotation it is clear that
Whitman brings religion into vital connection with the supreme subject of *Leaves of Grass*—the personality. Still clearer
is this from a significant suggestion in "Democratic Vistas":
"[Poetry] must place in the van, and hold up at all hazards, the
banner of the divine pride of man in himself, (the radical foundation of the new religion.)" [30] It is this divine pride, this
consciousness of divinity, that inspired Whitman, and which he
wished to see strengthened in men generally. In this way he
proposed to make religion one of the main buttresses of the
personality. It need scarcely be said that every religious thinker
deserving the name has done the same. By bringing the individual soul into some relation with the Highest; by effecting
some connection between the individual life and immortality;
by giving the pariah soul of man some status in that kingdom
of God, which embodies man's highest ethical and spiritual conceptions, the importance of the individual is indefinitely increased and the forces that sustain his inward progress are
indefinitely multiplied. Now religion in all its higher forms
teaches that man is a portion of the Eternal, an image of the
Highest, a manifestation of that cosmic spirit. And it is in the
practical application of this doctrine to human character and
personality that Whitman found the most important instru-
ment of human progress.

In one respect, however, his teaching differed from that of
most religious thinkers: he refused to recognise that the devil
had any share in the making or marring of man. As his belief in
the sanity and harmony of the cosmos enabled him to thread to
his satisfaction *des Lebens labyrinthisch irren Lauf* [31] and to

discover peace behind the warfare of appearance, so it enabled him also to banish all anomalies and singularities from his theology. The historic deadly feud between the powers of good and evil resolved itself into the dust clouds that accompany the invisible tread of the forces of progress.[32] Good and evil became, not causes inherent in the constitution of the universe, but modes of moral activity—effects accompanying the activity of non-moral causes within the narrow area marked off by pleasure and pain.[33] It seems that from his earliest years he was unable to grasp the idea of a contention waged between the powers of good and evil.

> Silent and amazed even when a little boy
> I remember I heard the preacher every Sunday put God
>   in his statements,
> As contending against some being or influence.[34]

His own mind being so harmonious and pacific, and his development having been so equable and continuous, the very idea of such a feud, as all systems of theology attest, seemed alien to his nature. No wonder that in later life, he effects, in "Chanting the Square Deific", a combination of ideas which might seem blasphemous to some people. To him the great dynamic behind phenomena, propelling the vast machinery of existence along the lines of evolution, has four sides or aspects: "Jehovah", whose activity is summed up by the inexorable law of cause and effect, operating within the moral world as the law of retribution and justice; "Christ", whose boundless mercy and sympathy and self-sacrifice temper the rigour of justice; "Satan", with his defiance and hatred and uncompromising insubordination, embodying the anarchic element; and "Santa Spirita", whose radiant and beneficent activities embrace and fill all existence, as the impalpable ether washes and pervades the whole universe. Such is the significant composition that Whitman effects of the ultimate world-forces.

One other element of Whitman's religious belief, also mentioned in the line italicised above, must here be referred to because of the striking light it throws on the vital connection, in

his mind, of personality and religion. This is his passionate belief in immortality, in the indestructibility of the identified
personality. Thus he says in "To Think of Time", published in
1855:

And I have dream'd that the purpose and essence of the known
    life, the transient,
Is to form and decide identity for the unknown life, the permanent.

If all came but to ashes of dung,
If maggots and rats ended us, then Alarum! for we are betray'd,
Then indeed suspicion of death.

Do you suspect death? If I were to suspect death I should die
    now.
Do you think I could walk pleasantly and well-suited toward
    annihilation? [35]

It is a significant fact that this impression in favour of immortality has always been strongest in those who possessed the
greatest and most virile personalities. As self-respect characterises the pure in life; as self-confidence marks the strong in
body and mind, so the belief in immortality naturally and almost unconsciously springs up in the strong soul—is but the
soul's spontaneous belief in its own inherent strength and
vitality. This intuition of personal indestructibility is on the
same footing as all other intuitions: it may be right, it may be
wrong, but it cannot be proved to be either the one or the
other. The soul may believe, the will may assent, but the intellect cannot fathom. The objective basis of our spiritual aspirations and ideals—the vague suggestions and intuitions
which, arising from the depths of our emotional and spiritual
personality, spread their ethereal haze over the horizon which
bounds mortal life and vision, and display those phenomena of
light and shade which fringe the dark outskirts of the world
beyond—lies beyond knowledge and proof. To dismiss these
impressions as mere illusions, because their objective validity
cannot be proved, is to display not only a certain shallowness
of nature, but also an ignorance of true science. All the phe-

nomena of life teach us that no centre of life stands isolated and unrelated; every such centre has its own environment, essential to its existence and evolution. The spiritual personality, too, needs its environment, and those intuitions and hopes and aspirations (which the shallow and the ignorant dismiss as mere illusions) form the natural environment of the soul or the spiritual personality, in which alone it can attain to a higher life; in which alone it can rend the fetters that arrest its progress and pursue its lone way along the yet unknown paths that mark the future evolution of cosmic life.

The Social Personality

We have now seen the main features of Whitman's individual personality. It is anarchistic; bent on progress at all hazards; for equality within the natural limits; averse to such moral distinctions as are traceable to social exigencies, and intensely spiritual.

It is obvious that, if these were the only constituent elements in the personality, man would be a most unhappy creature. For one thing, he would be doomed to tread for ever and unrestingly the thorny road of personal evolution. He could have no rest or peace, but would be for ever spurred on by the passion of progress. But to preserve him from this treadmill process a beneficent nature has added some other elements to his constitution. These elements make man a social being, and at once prompt and satisfy the requirements of social existence. The untrammelled operation of the individual personality as portrayed in "Song of Myself" would inevitably lead to "Chaos and Death". But as Whitman exclaims near the end of that poem:

Do you see, O my brothers and sisters?
It is not chaos or death—it is form, union, plan,—it is eternal
    life—it is Happiness.[36]

It remains, therefore, to consider the elements that constitute the social personality and secure the life and happiness of the individual and society.

Within the purview of *Leaves of Grass* there are four stages in the process by which the individual can transcend the painful limits of his narrow self and enter the objective world around him. These are supplied by the four capacities of sex, of comradeship, of nationality, and of spiritual idealism. Only the first three will be considered in this chapter.

▶ *Sex*

One feels a certain diffidence or hesitancy in approaching Whitman's treatment of the subject of sex, not because it is a hard or repellent subject, but because it is the one on which he has been most persistently misunderstood and misrepresented. In his own lifetime it brought him a rich harvest of obloquy and hatred; it brought him once at least within measurable distance of the criminal courts of his state; and even now it still seems to keep him outside the pale of polite literature. Too haughty to knock in the ordinary way at the doors of the "proud libraries"; too outspoken and coarse to make his presence acceptable to the belletristic drawing rooms of the world, he wanders mournfully about, like some branded Cain, the associate of his own pride and loneliness. Such has been the fate of him who devoted all his marvellous gifts to what seemed to him to be the highest service of his loved America, and finally sacrificed himself on the altar of that service; who tried to justify the ways of God with man even in those mysterious regions from which the heroism of the bravest has hitherto quailed. Such is the irony of fate: perhaps 'tis better so. I have seen the *Kreutzer Sonata* of Tolstoy exposed for sale in a window among obscene and immoral books intended to pander to the vices of the licentious. What a company for the ethical critic of Western civilisation, the lofty and spiritual interpreter of primitive Christianity! And where Tolstoy has found such strange and unexpected accommodation, what wonder that the far more outspoken Whitman has become a beacon of warning, a veritable Salt Pillar, at sight of which the faithful Pilgrim makes the sign of the cross, and the burnished Pharisee lifts his oily head in complacent thanks! Let us, eschewing praise and blame alike, address ourselves to the humble task of trying to understand.

Whitman's treatment of the subject of sex in that section of *Leaves of Grass* which he calls "Children of Adam" is based on two assumptions—the one negative, the other positive. The negative assumption is that which we have already considered at great length in dealing with the individual personality; viz., the assumption of the absence of inherent evil from the constitution of the universe. The ideas of sex and passion have always been closely associated in the minds of moralists with that of moral depravity; sex has been looked upon as the fountainhead of that stream of crime and sin whose course has so deeply soiled human character and history. It is passion, they say, that originally alienated the human race from God; and it is passion that still wars most effectively against the spiritual life of the soul.

Whitman refuses to believe in this inherent depravity of our sexual nature. What is natural to our physical constitution cannot be immoral in its normal operation. It is in the abnormal and excessive and unnatural operation of our impulses that the error lies; not in those impulses themselves. All excess is unnatural and sinful, as our physical nature shows by recoiling from it in lassitude and disgust; but what is natural cannot be sinful. As Goethe very elegantly puts it:

> *Alle menschliche Gebrachen*
> *Sühnet reiner Menschlichkeit.*[37]

The beautiful idea of St. Paul that the body is the temple of the Holy Spirit is adapted practically by Whitman and made the foundation of his views on sexual morality:

If any thing is sacred the human body is sacred,
And the glory and sweet of a man is the token of manhood
    untainted,
And in man or woman a clean, strong, firm-fibred body, is more
    beautiful than the most beautiful face.

Have you seen the fool that corrupted his own live body? or the
    fool that corrupted her own live body?

For they do not conceal themselves, and cannot conceal themselves.[38]

Stated in this way, most people will probably assent to Whitman's assumption as perfectly reasonable. And yet the current maxims and rules of morality are based exactly on the opposite assumption. The assumption on which monastic celibacy is founded has taken too deep religious roots in popular thought to be eradicated in the course even of centuries.

Besides this assumption that there is nothing depraved or wrong in the natural functions of the human body, Whitman makes another, which will be more readily assented to. In Whitman's view, sex is the foundation and starting point of all that is most noble in human character, most inspiring in human activity, and most precious to society. Take sex away from human nature, "untune that string", and all the rest becomes a dismal discord; for it is exactly that elements in our complex constitution which harmonises all the others. As long as there is any beauty in the passionate attachment of lovers and in the life-long fidelity of husband and wife; as long as pure unconscious children beam upon our soiled world and weary society; as long as youth cherishes dreams of the ideal; in short, as long as the human race continues to possess religion, art, poetry, and all that lifts us above the level of material existence, so long sex will remain the central fact and basis of our civilisation. Its subtle electricity braces human effort and purpose for the highest deeds; our highest ideas and ideals are ultimately the flowerings of this despised stalk. Take away sex and the most degrading materialism becomes the only possible alternative for the human race. Hence the importance of sex within the purview of *Leaves of Grass*.

Besides these two assumptions there were other considerations which led Whitman to give such prominence to the subject of sex in his work. As he had chosen the complete human being as his subject, he had to give full expression to his view.

. . . that the sexual passion in itself, while normal and unperverted, is inherently legitimate, creditable, not necessarily an improper theme for poet, as confessedly not for scientist—that, with reference to the whole construction, organism, and intentions of "Leaves of Grass", anything short of confronting that theme, and making myself clear upon it, as the enclosing basis of everything, (as the sanity of everything was to be the atmosphere of the poems,) I should beg the question in its most momentous aspect, and the superstructure that follow'd, pretensive as it might assume to be, would all rest on a poor foundation, or no foundation at all. In short, as the assumption of the sanity of birth, Nature and humanity, is the key to any true theory of life and the universe—at any rate, the only theory out of which I wrote—it is, and must inevitably be, the only key to "Leaves of Grass" and every part of it.[39]

To all this the ordinary prudent citizen will say, "Very well, all this is excellent theory. But are you justified in proclaiming it aloud from the housetops? Is it not expedient to suppress many a truth simply because its proclamation is more likely to do harm than good? And is not sex exactly one of these subjects on which it is expedient to preserve a religious silence outside the hospital and scientific laboratory?"

It is on this point of expediency that Whitman joins issue with the citizen aforesaid. In his opinion, "most of the ill births, inefficient maturity, snickering pruriency and of that human pathologic evil and morbidity which is the keel and reason-why of every evil and morbidity" is ultimately traceable to this ignorance on the topic that most vitally concerns all. Salvation for society lies only in letting the light fall fully and unreservedly on this dark topic; light is knowledge, and knowledge is power.

The time seems to me to have arrived, and America to be the place, for a new departure. The same freedom and faith and earnestness which, after centuries of denial, struggle, repression, and martyrdom, the present day brings to the treatment of politics and religion, must work out a plan and standard on this subject, not so much for what is called society, as for thoughtfullest men and women, and thoughtfullest literature. The same spirit that marks the physiological author and demonstrator on these topics in his important field, I have thought necessary to be exemplified, for once, in another certainly not less important field.[40]

At present the youth of both sexes secretly gather their information about the facts of sex—sometimes fatally erroneous —in ways which naturally result in the association of sex with the ideas of impurity and depravity. But if the youthful mind were to learn from sane and noble writers the facts of physical maturity and thus became early imbued with the ideas of the greatness and sacredness of the subject, the dictates of ordinary prudence or morality would be reinforced by the sanctions of religion and social morality would be most materially promoted.

Such are the main considerations which underlie Whitman's treatment of sex in *Leaves of Grass*. Amid the stress and strain of our latter-day urbanised civilisation, and the consequent temptations to which the youth are exposed, he thought that a new departure was necessary in the interests of social morality. With the departure, as he practically inaugurated it in the "Children of Adam", many will not agree and still more will be in suspense; but that his object was high and noble will now be questioned by very few.

▶ *Comradeship*

In reviewing his life-work in 1876, Whitman wrote:

I also sent out *Leaves of Grass* to arouse and set flowing in men's and women's hearts, young and old, (my present and future readers,) endless streams of living, pulsating love and friendship, directly from them to myself, now and ever. To this terrible, irrepressible yearning (surely more or less down underneath in most human souls,)— this never-satisfied appetite for sympathy, and this boundless offering of sympathy—this universal democratic comradeship—this old, eternal, yet ever-new interchange of adhesiveness, so fitly emblematic of America—I have given in that book, undisguisedly, declaredly, the openest expression.[41]

It is this beautiful conception of comradeship and the attractive forms in which that conception is expressed in the "Calamus" section of *Leaves of Grass* that have won for Whitman such a warm place in the hearts of most of his admirers.

In our materialist-scientific century such a conception, based not upon its economic or other worldly value, but expressive of the deepest needs of the human heart, is unique. Since the time of Christ no teacher of humanity has come forward with such a pure and lofty idea of human relations, and with the exception of Christ none has attached equal importance to love as the great renovative power in human destiny. It is therefore of the greatest interest to see what that conception of Whitman's was at this stage of his development. So far as we can now judge from the evidence before us, Christ's conception of love seems always to have had a religious reference. His was that love which endured in the higher love. The disciples had to love one another, because they were all children of the heavenly Father. The heavenly love was the root and *raison d'être* of the earthly love.

With Whitman, on the other hand, love was, at this stage of his development, a purely and frankly human relation. It had no reference whatever to religious considerations. It was a human plant which under certain conditions sprang up spontaneously in the real human heart. He calls it very significantly "comradeship", and the section, "Calamus", in which this comradeship is celebrated follows the section "Children of Adam", in which the sexual passion is sung. This seems to suggest—and the suggestion is explicitly borne out by what Whitman says elsewhere—that in his mind comradeship was a higher emotion than that of sex. To adopt his peculiar nomenclature, adhesiveness is a purer and more spiritual form of love than amativeness. While comradeship has not the same strong physical basis in human nature as amativeness, it certainly has a greater ideal basis and in that sense is a higher emotion.

But there is probably another reason why Whitman put comradeship above sex. Marriage, the practical and legalised expression of the sexual instinct, is often—and in its most successful cases, always—accompanied by the partial sacrifice of one personality to the other. The happiest cases of wedded life are those in which, as Shakespeare shows and all experience confirms, the wife more or less merges her independent per-

sonality in that of her husband. On the other hand, pure comradeship, even between persons of the opposite sex, involves no
such sacrifice or mergence. The complications of our physical
nature do not come in to mar the pure delight of soul in soul.
As the mind grows brighter by gazing on truth, so the soul
grows larger by gazing on its comrade soul. The emotional personality, instead of finding satisfaction in being merged, as in
marriage, in some earthly Nirvana, finds it in a higher development in the congenial atmosphere of deep and true affection.

The feeling of comradeship amounted in Whitman to a real
passion. As he expresses it in "A Song of Joys": "O the joy of
that vast elemental sympathy which only the human soul is
capable of generating and emitting in steady and limitless
floods".[42] In him the passion of comradeship is the natural and
spontaneous expression of that flux capacity or emotional
plasticity which forms the tap-root of his personality. And the
intensity of that passion finds burning expression in "Calamus".
Thus, in a little poem in which he tells how doubt often filled
his mind and he heard continually the obstinate inward ques-
tionings as to the reality of our ideals and aspirations, he winds
up thus:

When he whom I love travels with me or sits a long while holding
    me by the hand,
When the subtle air, the impalpable, the sense that words and
    reason hold not, surround us and pervade us,

Then I am charged with untold and untellable wisdom, I am
    silent, I require nothing further,
I cannot answer the question of appearances or that of identity
    beyond the grave,
But I walk or sit indifferent, I am satisfied,
He ahold of my hand has completely satisfied me.[43]

And in another little poem he tells the "Recorders ages
hence" to

Publish my name and hang up my picture as that of the tenderest
    lover,
The friend the lover's portrait, of whom his friend his lover was
    fondest

Who was not proud of his songs, but of the measureless ocean of
    love within him, and freely pour'd it forth,
Who often walk'd lonesome walks thinking of his dear friends, his
    lovers,
Who pensive away from one he lov'd often lay sleepless and
    dissatisfied at night,
Who knew too well the sick, sick dread lest the one he lov'd
    might secretly be indifferent to him,
Whose happiest days were far away through fields, in woods, on
    hills, he and another wandering hand in hand, they twain
    apart from other men,
Who oft as he saunter'd the streets curv'd with his arm the
    shoulder of his friend, while the arm of his friend rested
    upon him also.[44]

These poems were published in 1860. Eleven years later, in a
fine little poem called "The Base of All Metaphysics", he celebrates love in a subdued spirit which shows how the years had
tempered his surging passion:

And now gentlemen,
A word I give to remain in your memories and minds,
As base and finalé too for all metaphysics.

(So to the students the old professor,
At the close of his crowded course.)

Having studied the new and antique, the Greek and Germanic
    systems,
Kant having studied and stated, Fichte and Schelling and Hegel,
Stated the lore of Plato, and Socrates greater than Plato,
And greater than Socrates sought and stated, Christ divine having
    studied long,
I see reminiscent today those Greek and Germanic systems,
See the philosophies all, Christian churches and tenets see,
Yet underneath Socrates clearly see, and underneath Christ the
    divine I see,
The dear love of man for his comrade, the attraction of friend to
    friend,
Of the well-married husband and wife, of children and parents,
Of city for city and land for land.[45]

Finally, it must be pointed out that not only for its own sake did Whitman lay such stress in *Leaves of Grass* on this sentiment and practice of comradeship. To him it seemed the most powerful dynamic agency in the moral renovation of a materialistic society. Thus, he says in a footnote in "Democratic Vistas":

It is to the development, identification, and general prevalence of that fervid comradeship, (the adhesive love, at least rivalling the amative love hitherto possessing imaginative literature, if not going beyond it,) that I look for the counter-balance and offset of our materialistic and vulgar American democracy, and for the spiritualization thereof. Many will say it is a dream, and will not follow my inferences: but I confidently expect a time when there will be seen, running like a half-hid warp through all the myriad audible and visible worldly interests of America, threads of manly friendship, fond and loving, pure and sweet, strong and life-long, carried to degrees hitherto unknown—not only giving tone to individual character, and making it unprecedentedly emotional, muscular, heroic, and refined, but having the deepest relations to general politics. I say democracy infers such loving comradeship, as its most inevitable twin or counterpart, without which it will be incomplete, in vain, and incapable of perpetuating itself.[46]

▶ *Democratic Nationality*

The third means whereby the personality is enabled to rise above its individual limits is nationality. It remains, therefore, briefly to examine the character of Whitman's conception of nationality at this period of his development.

We have seen that one of the main truths which Whitman resolved to defend, or rather to champion towards victory and general acceptance, was the fundamental importance of the individuality, the simple, separate person. But he was just as profoundly convinced that within the area of achieved evolution there was something else equally great and equally important; that the personality was an organic synthesis transcending in importance all its individual thoughts, products, functions in one fact: that beyond the individual there is a larger organic synthesis comprising all individuals in a living and continuous aggregate is another and no less noteworthy fact, advocated in *Leaves of Grass* with at least as much impassioned vigour as the former. The conception of the people as being not a collection of diverse and purely competitive units, but as a living organism with its own laws of life and growth, is perhaps the greatest achievement of the historical method in our century. The same conception is one of the most fundamental in Whitman's work. The germ of the conception was probably latent in his personality, while its content, its vividness, and reality resulted from his social experience and his profound probing of social life to its inner meaning and sustaining forces.

The social organism is not perfect, just as the human personality is not perfect. Both are tending towards ideal types not yet reached in the course of evolution; and the imperfections of both are looked upon as the indispensable means whereby progress towards those ideals is maintained and accelerated. In society the most ennobling and cohesive force is comradeship; and thus, in Whitman's view, the ideal society is the union of comrades. While social union is grounded in the physical necessities of the personality; and while society is thus founded on the impregnable rockbed of passion; while its early development is mainly due to competition and the struggle for life, its higher organic evolution depends upon the invisible spirit of comradeship.

Come, I will make the continent indissoluble,
I will make the most splendid race the sun ever shone upon,
I will make divine magnetic lands,
    With the love of comrades,
    With the life-long love of comrades.

I will plant companionship thick as trees along all the rivers of
    America, and along the shores of the great lakes, and all
    over the prairies,
I will make inseparable cities with their arms about each other's
    necks,
    By the love of comrades,
    By the manly love of comrades.[47]

It may seem strange that a poet with such an ideal conception of human society as Whitman should have been able to reconcile himself so easily to the imperfect one he found around him. But here we come again across that acceptivity, that profoundly sympathetic tolerance and that unconquerable patience which marked his personality so strongly. Could he be taking thought or by defying the hard and impregnable facts of the universe add one unit to the rate of progress? What cannot be changed must be accepted; and he who accepts with acquiescence is wiser than he who accepts under protest. The wise man's attitude towards the universe and especially towards human society is a compromise, is the compromise of compromises. Such was Whitman's attitude: in him compromise rose from a mere empirical practice to the highest and greatest of principles; its mild and beneficent activity reconciled the warring factions of principles and ideals. This is the spirit of the great realist; the attitude of the man who sees the ideal, not in the fleeting phantoms of fancy, but in the real and concrete.

From the above conception of the people as an organic unity, as a sort of larger personality, developing according to its own laws and forms, it follows at once that Whitman was a frank democratic; that he believed in democracy and in the part it is destined to play in the future evolution of society. Some may say that this does not follow immediately, that another premise is necessary before it is possible to arrive at a frank acceptance of democracy. They would, like Mazzini, interpolate the assumption that the people is divine, and would state the argument in this wise: the people is an organism developing under its own inevitable forms (of which the democratic is one); the people is divine; somehow it comes from God. Therefore, democracy comes from God and must be frankly accepted. But Whitman takes a far more daring standpoint, and his faith in democracy has nothing to do with the fiction of its divinity. He plainly intimates [48] that he would continue to believe in the people although it were uncertain whether it came from God or the devil! And in this there is really nothing strange. For as has been pointed out above in describing his ultimate attitude

on all such questions, that his one fundamental conviction—
one springing from the very form of his personality—was that
the universe was at bottom sound; that its processes were really
sane and healthy; and that democracy as one of these processes
was in spite of its extravagances and shortcomings at bottom
sound and good. It is good in the same deep sense that the old
chronicler noted: "And God overlooked all he had made and
saw that it was good".

From this it is obvious that Whitman does not believe in an
abstract democracy; with him it must be a real concrete phenomenon; and the question whether any nationality has developed the capacity which fits it for popular self-government
is a practical one, which must be decided on the historical facts
of each case.

While Whitman thus calmly accepted democracy as a fact,
and as in many senses a beneficent fact, he was not unaware of
its weaknesses and dangers. Yet on a careful review of his work
published before the American war it becomes evident that
Whitman accepted democracy with too much complacency; that
he did not sufficiently distinguish between its inevitable draw-
backs and its undoubted advantages. In fact, his belief in
democracy seems to me to have been based at this time more on
his cheerful recognition of it as an accomplished fact than on
a due appreciation of its advantages and disadvantages. His
later experience was, as will shortly be seen, to affect very materially this aspect of his opinions.

The other ground why Whitman's attachment to the democratic creed at this period was so undivided and undiluted by
any misgivings was that he identified democracy with the mission of his own beloved America. How could the political
method of the people that was to give a new character to the
advancing civilisation of humanity be radically wrong? Thus
his appreciative reading of his own people supplied him with
a brief for democracy. And the following apostrophe to democracy—which, though written at a much later date, really
reflects his opinions of this period—was in fact addressed to
the United States of America:

Sail, sail thy best, ship of Democracy,
Of value is thy freight, 'tis not the Present only,
The Past is also stored in thee,
Thou holdest not the venture of thyself alone, not of the Western
    continent alone,
Earth's *résume* entire floats on thy keel O ship, is steadied by
    thy spars,
With thee Time voyages in trust, the antecedent nations suck or
    swim with thee,
With all their ancient struggles, martyrs, heroes, epics, wars,
    thou bear'st the other continents,
Theirs, theirs as much as thine, the destination-port triumphant;
Steer then with good strong hand and wary eye, O helmsman; thou
    carriest great companions,
Venerable priestly Asia sails this day with thee,
And royal feudal Europe sails with thee.[49]

How he came to read democracy much more profoundly by the
light of his later experience; how he criticised it; what practical
suggestions he had to offer for its future development; and what
his ultimate conception of democracy was, will be fully shown
in later sections of this work.

5

Period of Emotionalism
(1862-1865)

The War

IN A remarkable passage of *Wilhelm Meister,* which Carlyle has made familiar to the English world, Goethe points out that the most distinctive feature of the Christian religion is the place it assigns to sorrow in the culture of the spiritual life. The dark forms in which sorrow clothes herself and moves among mankind are not, in the opinion of the Christ, to be regarded with philosophic indifference or superstitious fear. They are the means whereby the rebellious, discontented, selfish individual is disciplined to a higher life. They alone can mould the murmur of the individual voices into the harmony of a progressive humanity. And Goethe himself has given expression to this high function of sorrow and suffering in those memorable lines:

> *Wer nie sein Brot mit Thränen ass,*
> *Wer nie die kummervollen Nächte*
> *Auf seinem Bette weinend sass,*
> *Der kennt euch nicht, ihr himmlischen Mächte.*[1]

We shall now have an opportunity of studying the far-reaching influence which sorrow and suffering had in the development of Whitman's personality.

We left him in the last chapter at a very remarkable stage in his development. The period between 1855 and 1861, between

101

the publication of *Leaves of Grass* and the beginning of the American Civil War, saw Whitman at the very height of his manhood. Physically, intellectually, and aesthetically he had arrived at the high-water mark of his development. His appearance seems to have been of the most striking character. It is during the early years of the war that W. D. O'Connor drew his picture from life with such striking effect:

For years past, thousands of people in New York, in Brooklyn, in Boston, in New Orleans, and latterly in Washington, have seen, even as I saw two hours ago, tallying, one might say, the streets of our American cities, and fit to have for his background and accessories, their streaming populations and ample and rich façades, a man of striking masculine beauty—a poet—powerful and venerable in appearance; large, calm, superbly formed; oftenest clad in the careless, rough, and always picturesque costume of the common people; resembling and generally taken by strangers for, some great mechanic or stevedore, or seaman, or grand laborer of one kind or another; and passing slowly in this guise, with nonchalant and haughty step along the pavement, with the sunlight and shadows falling around him. The dark sombrero he usually wears was, when I saw him just now, the day being warm, held for the moment in his hand; rich light an artist would have chosen, lay upon his uncovered head, majestic, large, Homeric, and set upon his strong shoulders with the grandeur of ancient sculpture; I marked the countenance, serene, proud, cheerful, florid, grave; the brow seamed with noble wrinkles; the features, massive and handsome, with firm blue eyes; the eyebrows and eyelids especially showing that fullness of arch seldom seen save in the antique busts; the flowing hair and fleecy beard, both very gray, and tempering with a look of age the youthful aspect of one who is but forty-five; the simplicity and purity of his dress, cheap and plain, but spotless, from snowy falling collar to burnished boot, and exhaling faint fragrance; the whole form surrounded with manliness as with a nimbus, and breathing, in its perfect health and vigor, the august charm of the strong.[2]

Such was his outward appearance. As for the texture and composition of his mind, we have examined that at full length. If one may venture to sum up all his characteristics at this time and express them in one term, it will probably be pride

—pride in a high and noble sense—but still pride. It is the conscious self-sufficiency of the personality at the height of its physical and intellectual maturity. Probably the spirit of the following passage, taken from the Preface to the first edition of *Leaves of Grass,* will indicate more accurately than any words of mine could do the general attitude and position of Whitman at this stage of his development:

All beauty comes from beautiful blood and a beautiful brain. If the greatnesses are in conjunction in a man or woman, it is enough . . . . the fact will prevail through the universe . . . . but the gaggery and gilt of a million years will not prevail. Who troubles himself about his ornaments or fluency is lost. This is what you shall do: Love the earth and sun and the animals, despise riches, give alms to every one that asks, stand up for the stupid and crazy, devote your income and labor to others, hate tyrants, argue not concerning God, have patience and indulgence toward the people, take off your hat to nothing known or unknown or to any man or number of men, go freely with powerful uneducated persons and with the young and with the mothers of families, read these leaves in the open air every season of every year of your life, re-examine all you have been told at school or church or in any book, dismiss whatever insults your own soul and your very flesh shall be a great poem and have the richest fluency not only in its words but in the silent lines of its lips and face and between the lashes of your eyes and in every motion and joint of your body.[3]

It is a high and noble code; but it lacks one thing—the one thing needful for entry into the kingdom of heaven—it lacks humility. It is obvious that the man who drafted this code had not been in the school of sorrow; he had never eaten his bread with tears; he had never felt the sense of tears in all things mortal. No doubt had yet been allowed to mark the categorical sufficiency of his creed; no cloud-speck had yet dimmed his radiant faith in man, in his country, in the cosmos.

But the war of 1861–1865, with its terrible experiences for Whitman, was to bring about a remarkable change in the temper and attitude of his mind. In some sense the change may be said to have been almost revolutionary. And yet, if one looks at the matter carefully, it becomes clear that there was no revolution; the mind did not strike out a new path, only its mode of action and motion was deeply influenced by the new experience.

It may be an idle question to ask, and yet it is interesting to consider what the future development of Whitman might and probably would have been, but for the war's contribution to his experience. Many passages may be quoted to show that even before the war his mind was beginning to rise above the level of naturalism already described. Already its aspirations were beginning to be directed towards the ideal. True, this ideal was not far off, removed beyond the real and actual; it was inherent in the real.

It is clear that the spiritual germ was already actively stirring in his mind; and even in the absence of the war experiences it would have leavened his thought till ultimately his standpoint would have been that of religious spiritualism which he actually did reach. But it is equally clear that the rich human note, the timbre of sorrow, in which his rough music excels that of all other poets, would have been far less striking in the final result if he had not probed the depths of sorrow and suffering as he did during the war.

On 13 April 1861, the attack on Fort Sumter signalised the real beginning of the war; a few months later it had become quite general. One of Whitman's brothers was an officer in the Federal army, and the news of the injuries he had sustained in battle brought Whitman to the hospitals at Washington. It was towards the end of 1862 that his attendance at the hospitals as an informal nurse became quite regular; and it remained so till the end of the war in the summer of 1865.

We have two sets of documents recording the experiences through which he was now passing and their effect on his thought. We have the section of *Leaves of Grass* which begins with "Drum Taps" and closes with the "Memories of President Lincoln". But independently of this we have *Specimen Days,* which arose out of little memoranda, originally jotted down by Whitman at the very time of the events they recorded.

These two sets of evidence afford unusual opportunities of studying the strata of experience through which Whitman's personality was now cutting its way. It will be advisable here to make Whitman speak for himself as far as possible, as it will be impossible to improve on the vividness and accuracy of his own unvarnished accounts.

During this stay at Washington he supported himself chiefly by journalism; and partly with his own earnings, and with funds kindly forwarded by his friends for that purpose, he was able to supply patients with little necessaries and luxuries.

In regard to his hospital visits he says:

In my visits to the hospital I found it was in the simple matter of personal presence, and emanating ordinary cheer and magnetism, that I succeeded and help'd more than by medical nursing, or delicacies, or gifts of money, or anything else. During the war I possess'd the perfection of physical health. My habit, when practicable, was to prepare for starting out on one of those daily or nightly tours of from a couple to four or five hours, by fortifying myself with previous rest, the bath, clean clothes, a good meal, and as cheerful an appearance as possible.[4]

I shall now simply quote a number of illustrative passages from these memoranda:

I am now remaining in and around Washington, daily visiting the hospitals. Am much in Patent-office, Eighth street, H street, Armory-square and others. Am now able to do a little good, having money, (as almoner of others home,) and getting experience. Today, Sunday afternoon and till nine in the evening, visited Campbell hospital; attended especially to one case in ward 1, very sick with pleurisy and typhoid fever, young man, farmer's son, D. F. Russell, company E, 60th New York, downhearted and feeble; a long time before he would take any interest; wrote a letter home to his mother, in Malone, Franklin county, N. Y., at his request; gave him some fruit and one or two other gifts; envelop'd and directed his letter, etc. Then went thoroughly through ward 6, observ'd every case in the ward, without, I think, missing one; gave perhaps from twenty to thirty persons, each one some little gift, such as oranges, apples, sweet crackers, figs, etc.[5]

When eligible, I encourage the men to write, and myself, when called upon, write all sorts of letters for them, (including love letters, very tender ones.) [6]

You may hear groans or other sounds of unendurable suffering from two or three of the cots, but in the main there is quiet—almost a painful absence of demonstration; but the pallid face, the dull'd eye, and the moisture on the lip, are demonstration enough. Most of these sick or hurt are evidently young fellows from the country, farmers' sons, and such like. Look at the fine large frames, the bright and broad countenances, and the many yet lingering proofs of strong constitution and physique. Look at the patient and mute manner of our American wounded as they lie in such a sad collection. [7]

This afternoon, July 22d, I have spent a long time with Oscar F. Wilber, company G, 154th New York, low with chronic diarrhoea, and a bad wound also. He asked me to read him a chapter in the New Testament. I complied, and ask'd him what I should read. He said, "Make your own choice." I open'd at the close of one of the first books of the evangelists, and read the chapters describing the latter hours of Christ, and the scenes at the crucifixion. The poor, wasted young man ask'd me to read the following chapter also, how Christ rose again. I read very slowly, for Oscar was feeble. It pleased him very much, yet the tears were in his eyes. He ask'd me if I enjoy'd religion. I said, "Perhaps not, my dear, in the way you mean, and yet, may-be, it is the same thing." He said, "It is my chief reliance." He talk'd of death, and said he did not fear it. I said, "Why, Oscar, don't you think you will get well?" He said, "I may, but it is not probable." He spoke calmly of his condition. The wound was very bad; it discharg'd much. Then the diarrhoea had prostrated him, and I felt that he was even then the same as dying. He behaved very manly and affectionate. The kiss I gave him as I was about leaving he return'd fourfold. He gave me his mother's address . . . . He died a few days after the one just described. [8]

Soldiers, soldiers, soldiers, you meet everywhere about the city, often superb-looking men, though invalids dress'd in worn uniforms, and carrying canes and crutches. I often have talks with them, occasionally quite long and interesting. One, for instance, will have been all through the peninsula under McClellan—narrates to me the fights, the marches, the strange, quick changes of that eventful campaign, and gives glimpses of many things untold in any official reports or books or journals. These, indeed, are the things that are genuine and precious. The man was there, has been out two years, has been through a dozen fights, the superfluous flesh of talking is long work'd off him, and he gives me little but the hard meat and sinew . . . . I now doubt whether one can get a fair idea of what this war practically is, or what genuine America is, and her character, without some such experience as this I am having.[9]

It is curious: when I am present at the most appalling scenes, deaths, operations, sickening wounds (perhaps full of maggots,) I keep cool and do not give out or budge, although my sympathies are very much excited; but often, hours afterward, perhaps when I am home, or out walking alone, I feel sick, and actually tremble, when I recall the case again before me.[10]

Of scenes like these, I say, who writes—who e'er can write the story? Of many a score—aye, thousands, north and south, of unwrit heroes, unknown heroisms, incredible, impromptu, first-class desperations—who tells? No history ever—no poem sings, no music sounds, those bravest men of all—those deeds. No formal general's report, nor book in the library, nor column in the paper, embalms the bravest, north or south, east or west. Unnamed, unknown remain, and still remain, the bravest soldiers. Our manliest—our boys —our hardy darlings; no picture gives them. Likely, the typic one of them (standing, no doubt, for hundreds, thousands,) crawls aside to some bush-clump, or ferny tuft, on receiving his death-shot— there sheltering a little while, soaking roots, grass and soil, with red blood—the battle advances, retreats, flits from the scene, sweeps by—and there, haply with pain and suffering (yet less, far less, than is supposed,) the last lethargy winds like a serpent round him—the eyes glaze in death—none recks—perhaps the burial-squads, in truce, a week afterwards, search not the secluded spot—and there, at last, the Bravest Soldier crumbles in mother earth, unburied and unknown.[11]

And finally he thus sums up his war experiences:

During those three years in hospital, camp or field, I made over six hundred visits or tours, and went, as I estimate, counting all, among from eighty thousand to a hundred thousand of the wounded and sick, as sustainer of spirit and body in some degree, in time of need. These visits varied from an hour or two, to all day or night; for with dear or critical cases I generally watch'd all night. Sometimes I took up my quarters in the hospital, and slept or watch'd there several nights in succession. Those three years I consider the greatest privilege and satisfaction (with all their feverish excitements and physical deprivations and lamentable sights,) and, of course, the most profound lesson of my life. I can say that in my ministerings I comprehended all, whoever came in my way, northern or southern, and slighted none. It arous'd and brought out and decided undream'd-of depths of emotion. It has given me my most fervent views of the true *ensemble* and extent of the States. While I was with wounded and sick in thousands of cases from the New England States, and from New York, New Jersey, and Pennsylvania, and from Michigan, Wisconsin, Ohio, Indiana, Illinois, and all the Western States, I was with more or less from all the States, North and South, without exception. I was with many from the border States, especially from Maryland and Virginia, and found, during those lurid years 1862–63, far more Union Southerners, especially Tennesseans, than is supposed. I was with many rebel officers and men among our wounded, and gave them always what I had, and tried to cheer them the same as any. I was among the army teamsters considerably, and, indeed, always found myself drawn to them. Among the black soldiers, wounded or sick, and in the contraband camps, I also took my way whenever in their neighborhood, and did what I could for them.[12]

Summing up the contributions of this period towards the growth of Whitman's personality, one may say that these records show advance in two directions: (1) while his experience of sorrow and suffering deepened his emotional humanity, it also carried them beyond humanity to idealism, and it is from this time that the ideal-spiritual element becomes conspicuous in his writings; (2) the idea of American nationality, as a source not only of political union, but also of spiritual strength, began to take definite shape in his mind. Let us look more closely at both these developments.

The Emotional Meridian: The Spiritual Dawn

I have already treated of Whitman's beautiful conception of comradeship—the conception of a new social world raised on the runis of feudalism and competitive industrialism, in which the cementing ties of society will be the primal affinities and attractions of human nature. Nothing can be nobler and lovelier than that conception as it appears in "Calamus". But if we turn to the poems written after the end of the Civil War, we find a far more subtle and profound appreciation of the sympathetic forces of human nature. The chords of his deeply sympathetic soul, wrung by the inexpressible sorrows and horrors of that war, developed a new resonance; they became capable of articulating that deeper, stiller music which springs from sorrow too deep for words, despair too great for sympathy. Human affection is great and strong. But there comes a period in the experience of the soul when, in the valley of the sunless shadow, even such affection ceases to attract. Then it is that the soul begins to apprehend the dim and fitful presence of a greater passion—a passion that ultimately carries it beyond natural humanity to the higher regions of the spiritual world. It is when our flesh-and-blood humanity thus passes into ideality, into divinity, that our affections become spiritualised, and we become filled with that divine sympathy which is not repelled but attracted all the more strongly by the hatred and injuries received from others. Through this period Whitman had passed, and his eyes were beginning to catch the rays of the sun that shines beyond human society. Note, for instance, the spirit of this very significant passage from *Specimen Days:*

Every now and then, in hospital or camp, there are beings I meet —specimens of unworldliness, disinterestedness, and animal purity and heroism—perhaps some unconscious Indianian, or from Ohio or Tennessee—on whose birth the calmness of heaven seems to have descended, and whose gradual growing up, whatever the circumstances of his work-life or change, or hardship, or small or no education that attended it, the power of a strange spiritual sweetness, fibre and inward health, have also attended. Something veil'd and abstracted is often a part of the manners of these beings. I have met them, I say, not seldom in the army, in camp, and in the hospitals. The Western regiments contain many of them. They are often young men, obeying the events and occasions about them, marching, soldiering, fighting, foraging, cooking, working on farms or at some trade before the war—unaware of their own nature, (as to that, who is aware of his own nature?), their companions only understanding that they are different from the rest, more silent, "Something odd about them," and apt to go off and meditate and muse in solitude.[13]

It is obvious that the writer of this passage has made some advance on the writer of "Song of Myself". As further evidence of his development during this war-period, compare the following two passages, one taken from "Calamus", the other written at the conclusion of the war, and notice how much profounder the latter is than the former:

I dream'd in a dream I saw a city invincible to the attacks of the
 whole of the rest of the earth,
I dream'd it was the new city of Friends,
Nothing was greater there than the quality of robust love, it led
 the rest,
It was seen every hour in the actions of the men of that city,
And in all their looks and words.[14]

Contrast this with the following, written to commemorate the conclusion of the war:

Word over all, beautiful as the sky,
Beautiful that war and all its deeds of carnage must in time be
 utterly lost,
That the hands of the sisters Death and Night incessantly, softly
 wash again, and ever again, this soiled world;
For my enemy is dead, a man divine as myself is dead,
I look where he lies white-faced and still in the coffin—I draw
 near,
Bend down and touch lightly with my lips the white face in the
 coffin.[15]

Both passages are intended to celebrate the power of human affection and sympathy; yet what profounder passion and insight there slumber in the later one! It is obvious that a gulf of experience separates the two passages. The exultant optimist of "Calamus" had become a man of sorrows and acquainted with grief. While the earlier poem is inspired by a noble humanitarian passion, the later one breathes, more distinctly than any passage to be found elsewhere in literature, the divine spirit of the Christ.

Or take again the following lines, written indeed at a somewhat later date, but which show how much more profound and sweet and spiritual his passion of sympathy had become in consequence of his experience in the war:

Sweet are the blooming cheeks of the living—sweet are the
    musical voices sounding,
But sweet, ah sweet, are the dead with their silent eyes.

Dearest Comrades, all is over and long gone,
But love is not over—and what love, O Comrades!
Perfume from battlefields rising, up from the factor arising.

Perfume therefore my chant, O love, immortal love,
Give me to bathe the memories of all dead soldiers,
Shroud them, embalm them, cover them all over with tender pride.

Perfume all—make all wholesome,
Make these ashes to nourish and blossom,
O love, solve all, fructify all with the last chemistry.

Give me exhaustless, make me a fountain,
That I exhale love from me wherever I go like a moist perennial
    dew,
For the ashes of all dead soldiers South or North.[16]

But the poem which shows more significantly than any other the great effect of the war on Whitman's emotional power and expression is the ode on Lincoln's death, "When Lilacs Last in the Dooryard Bloom'd", certainly the masterpiece among his poetical compositions, and in some respects matchless in the whole history of literature. Even at the risk of introducing a digression, a short analysis of this poem must here be made, since both its general method and some of its leading ideas throw a great light on Whitman's personality and its development.

Many passages in *Specimen Days* testify with what reverence and grateful admiration Whitman regarded Lincoln. Here is an extract from the memorandum written on the assassination:

He leaves for America's history and biography, so far, not only its most dramatic reminiscence—he leaves, in my opinion, the greatest, best, most characteristic, artistic, moral personality. Not but that he had faults, and show'd them in the Presidency; but honesty, goodness, shrewdness, conscience, and (a new virtue, unknown to other lands, and hardly yet really known here, but the foundation and tie of all, as the future will grandly develop,) *Unionism*, in its truest and amplest sense, form'd the hard-pan of his character. These he seal'd with his life. The tragic splendor of his death, purging, illuminating all, throws round his form, his head, an aureole that will remain and will grow brighter through time, while history lives, and love of country lasts. By many has this Union been help'd; but if one name, one man, must be pick'd out, he, most of all, is the conservator of it, to the future. He was assassinated—but the Union is not assassinated—*ça ira!* One falls, and another falls. The soldier drops, sinks like a wave—but the ranks of the ocean eternally press on. Death does its work, obliterates a hundred, a thousand—President, general, captive, private—but the Nation is immortal.[17]

The tension of his emotional nature had already become too great in consequence of what he had seen in the course of the war; and when the assassination of America's greatest son and conservator came crowning the dread list of horrors, his soul overflowed in that moving hymn. All his long poems pretend to be something more than mere poems. Some are prophetic, others political; others expound new theories of religion, ethics, or literature. But this great hymn is a cry of pure passion, wrung from the soul. In it Whitman rose above all theories and roles into that serener ether of passion in which, alone, the highest poetry becomes possible.

On looking at this poem one is struck at once by the fact that the whole construction depends on a few simple ideas or poetic hinges. The evening star, the hermit thrush, the lilac tree, the death of Lincoln: such are the simple elements from which the whole is constructed. At first the mind is puzzled why just these elements—at least the first three—were chosen. But on reading *Specimen Days* [18] one sees the explanation! There we find memoranda recording the facts that the brilliance of Venus was for some time before the end of the war so striking as to be a topic of general discussion and admiration; also, that the lilac trees, which were in full bloom at the time of the assassination, had even a stronger scent than usual; also, that at this time— probably owing to his overwrought nervous condition—Whitman was often sleepless and passed the nights in the woods, listening to the song of the thrushes and watching the unwontedly brilliant Venus. Here, then, we have the imagery of the poem: no obscure classical figures and personages; no abstract scientific conceptions; but the simple facts of Whitman's contemporaneous experience.

The poem consists of sixteen numbered stanzas of varying length. The first introduces to us three of the *momenta* of the poem.

When lilacs last in the dooryard bloom'd,
And the great star early droop'd in the western sky in the night,
I mourn'd, and yet shall mourn with ever-returning spring.

Ever-returning spring, trinity sure to me you bring,
Lilac blooming perennial and drooping star in the west,
And thought of him I love.

In the second stanza the "powerful western fallen star" appears, attracting the poet's soul with some mysterious influence.

In the third, he returns to the lilac and describes it with characteristic detail:

In the dooryard fronting an old farm-house near the white-washed
    palings,

Stands the lilac-bush tall-growing with the heart-shaped leaves of
   rich green,
With many a pointed blossom, rising delicate, with the perfume
   strong I love,
With every leaf a miracle—and from this bush in the dooryard,
With delicate-color'd blossoms and heart-shaped leaves of rich
   green,
A sprig with its flower I break.

In the fourth stanza the thrush appears, the shy and hidden
bird, warbling the "Song of the bleeding throat, / Death's outlet song of life", in the secluded recesses of the swamp.

In the fifth, the coffin appears, journeying night and day over
the land; and in the sixth, its progress is described:

Coffin that passes through lanes and streets,
Through day and night with the great cloud darkening the land,
With the pomp of the inloop'd flags, with the cities draped in black,
With the show of the States themselves as of crape-veil'd women
   standing,
With processions long and winding and the flambeaus of the night,
With the countless torches lit, with the silent sea of faces and the
   unbared heads,
. . . .
With the tolling, tolling bells' perpetual clang,
Here, coffin that slowly passes
I give you my sprig of lilac.

In the seventh, the poet says that the sprig is laid on the
coffin not for Lincoln alone, but for all who died in the war.

In the eighth, the poet returns to the western orb sailing the
heaven, and says that now he sees why it held him with such
mysterious power as he walked "in silence the transparent
shadowy night".

In the ninth, he returns to the thrush, the singer bashful and
tender; and in the tenth, he asks:

O how shall I warble myself for the dead one there I loved?
And how shall I deck my song for the large sweet soul that has gone?
And what shall my perfume be for the grave of him I love?

He answers that his song will be the seawinds from the Pacific and the Atlantic, meeting on the prairies, and mixed "with the breath of my chant".

Then, in the eleventh stanza he asks what pictures he ought to hang on the chamber walls "to adorn the burial-house of him I love?" And in answer he unrolls a vast picture of America, rural and urban, lit by the sun as it travels from morn till eve:

Pictures of growing spring and farms and houses
With the Fourth-month eve at sundown, and the gray smoke
    lucid and bright,
With floods of the yellow gold of the gorgeous, indolent, sinking
    sun, burning, expanding the air,
With the fresh sweet herbage under foot, and the pale green leaves
    of the trees prolific,
In the distance the flowing glaze, the breast of the river, with a
    wind-dapple here and there,
With ranging hills on the banks, with many a line against the sky,
    and shadows,
And the city at hand with dwellings so dense, and stacks of chimneys,
And all the scenes of life and the workshops, and the workmen
    homeward returning.
Lo, the most excellent sun, so calm and haughty,
The violet and purple morn with just-felt breezes,
The gentle soft-born measureless light,
The miracle spreading bathing all, the fulfill'd noon,
The coming eve delicious, the welcome night and the stars,
Over my cities shining all, enveloping man and land.

In the fourteenth stanza the poet again addresses the thrush:

O liquid and free and tender!
O wild and loose to my soul—O wondrous singer!

He goes on to tell how he sat at dusk "in the large unconscious scenery of my land with its lakes and forests". The heaven was filled with an aerial beauty and all the land looked strange. Then there

Appear'd the cloud, appear'd the long black trail,[19]
And I knew death, its thought, and the sacred knowledge
 of death.

Then with the knowledge of death as walking one side of me,
And the thought of death close-walking the other side of me,
And I in the middle as with companions, and as holding the
 hands of companions,
I fled forth to the hiding receiving night that talks not,
Down to the shores of the water, the path by the swamp in the
 dimness,
To the solemn shadowy cedars and the ghostly pines so still.

  And there, as he listened to the sad melody of the thrush, his
own heart burst out responsive in a hymn to death:

Come lovely and soothing death,
Undulate round the world, serenely arriving, arriving,
In the day, in the night, to all, to each,
Sooner or later delicate death.

Prais'd be the fathomless universe,
For life and joy, and for objects and knowledge curious,
And for love, sweet love—but praise! praise! praise!
For the sure-enwinding arms of cool-enfolding death.

Dark mother always gliding near with soft feet,
Have none chanted for thee a chant of fullest welcome?
Then I chant it for thee, I glorify thee above all,
I bring thee a song that when thou must indeed come, come
 unfalteringly.

Approach, strong deliveress,
When it is so, when thou hast taken them I joyously sing the dead,
Lost in the loving floating ocean of thee,
Laved in the flood of thy bliss O death.

From me to thee glad serenades,
Dances for thee I propose saluting thee, adornments and
 feastings for thee,

And the sights of the open landscape and the high-spread sky are
*   fitting,*
And life and the fields, and the huge and thoughtful night.

The night in silence under many a star,
The ocean shore and the husky whispering wave whose voice I
*   know,*
And the soul turning to thee O vast and well-veil'd death,
And the body gratefully nestling close to thee.

Over the tree-tops I float thee a song,
Over the rising and sinking waves, over the myriad fields and the
*   prairies wide,*
Over the dense-pack'd cities all and the teeming wharves and ways,
I float this carol with joy, with joy to thee O death.

And as in unison with the chant of his soul, the grey-brown bird kept up loud and strong, "with pure deliberate notes spreading filling the night", long panoramas of visions unrolled before his sight. He saw the vast armies, moving and fighting; the heaps of the slain, who were beyond suffering; the groups of the living, the mother, the wife, the child, the musing comrade, who all remained to suffer.

And in the last stanza these panoramas fade away, the thrush goes to sleep, the western star sinks behind the horizon, and the poet ceases from his song and his communings. But he has a gift:

For the sweetest, wisest soul of all my days and lands—and this
    for his dear sake,
Lilac and star and bird twined with the chant of my soul,
There in the fragrant pines and the cedars dusk and dim.

Three observations I wish to make on this poem:

(1) Comparatively little space is devoted to Lincoln himself: in fact, he is only a few times alluded to. The special subject of his death is wrought up into that larger whole, which comprises all its real and imaginative surroundings. From the death of Lincoln the poet passes at once to the other deaths of the

war; and then again to death as a universal phenomenon. Thus we have here again a striking instance of Whitman's method of treating the individual not for its special so much as for its typical significance: the one is considered as indissolubly bound up with the whole.

(2) There is absolutely nothing hysterical about Whitman's sorrow. This is all the more remarkable when we recollect how terribly strung his whole system had become by his experiences; that he had already partly succumbed in 1864, and that his wonderful physique was as a consequence to be totally wrecked in 1873. How unutterably deep, and yet how pure and lofty, how healthy and sane is his sorrow! There is not a vestige in it of the morbid, the melancholy. This is partly due to the inherent sanity of his personality; partly—and perhaps mostly —to the all-embracive, all-connective quality referred to in (1). For notice how, with the thought of death, he links the thought of the huge and thoughtful night, of the husky whispering wave, of life, of the cities and prairies, and finally of the body gratefully nestling close to the bosom of the dark mother. These images of grandeur and sweetness are mingled with the thought of death, and as a consequence the poignancy of that thought passes away. Death becomes but a part of the mysterious, beautiful, and withal loveable All in which we live and move.

(3) And this brings us to Whitman's remarkable attitude to death. I have quoted the whole of the hymn to death, not only because it is a striking instance of the unsurpassed sublimity to which Whitman occasionally attains, but because it expresses so completely his own attitude towards death. He does not isolate the phenomenon and regard it in its natural repulsiveness as the King of Terrors. Starting from the ultimate postulate that life is imperishable—that the personality, having once arrived, never again disappears in all the aeons of progressive existence —he regards death as but one of the necessary steps in that endless progress. In the little piece called "Gods", which will be quoted in the last chapter, he even goes so far as to regard death as an object of religious worship; and in this hymn he clothes

her with such divine beauty and fascinating loveliness that she really appears as the sweet nurse-mother of humanity, lulling her troubled, storm-tossed children to rest on her mystic bosom.

Here we see the devoted nurse through whose hands a hundred thousand patients had passed. Here we see the lover of men who had absorbed into his great soul the sorrows and troubles, the pain and suffering, of his fellows, and who had found that they only deepened and broadened and purified the personality. But here we see also the great poet, the complete universal lover; the philosopher who refused to find in any nook or cranny of the vast whole anything that was unhealthy or anomalous; whose passion it was to see steadily the whole of the vast cosmos in the light of the idea of unity—a unity not merely mechanical, but mystic, spiritual, divine.[20]

And in the white heat of that cosmic passion, will death alone be incapable of fusion and harmonisation? The noblest vision of ancient poetic prophecy was that of death vanquished, of the universal captor led captive at last. And Whitman, too, sees that vision and feels its fascination. But reconciliation, not victory, is the keynote of his answer; underlies his solution of the world-old difficulty. Death is not for him the enemy vanquished, but the mystic friend recognised at last. The ancient faiths of the world have failed to rob death of its horrors for the popular mind. At most they have enabled a few favoured spirits to look undismayed on death, and to acquire from that look the immoveable steadfastness which refuses to be terrified. But there is a point of view, open to all alike, from which death appears as the great guardian of human happiness and progress. And in proportion as that point of view becomes more prominent, one of the most fertile sources of suffering to our race will dry up. He who has drunk in the spirit of this great hymn to death can never again look upon it otherwise than as the dark mother whose soft footsteps among mankind mark the end of pain and sorrow—the masked usher who opens to life's traveller the gates of the eternal kingdoms.

It is instructive to notice the evolution of Whitman's attitude towards death. At first it is not very different from the ordinary attitude. Thus he says in "Song of Myself": "And as to you Death, and you bitter hug of mortality, it is idle to try to alarm me".

Five years later, in "A Song of Joys", he speaks of the "Joys of the thought of Death"; and again of "the beautiful touch of Death".

Finally comes the war: its dread apocalypse of horror and suffering charged his idea of death with that deeper meaning and mystic passion, so conspicuous in the above hymn.

American Nationality

Having thus seen how his experience as a hospital nurse brought Whitman's emotional capacity to maturity, and how, from the height of his emotional manhood, he began to catch glimpses of the spiritual light that shines in the highest regions of the personality, it remains for us still to trace the other influence with which his war experiences are indissolubly bound up.

We have already seen how Whitman's conception of comradeship was also one of the bases of his conception of society. The society of the true friends of comrades was for him also the true and only city. But this was only an ideal; contact with the hard facts of reality, and especially his experience during the Union struggle of 1861–1865, were destined to give a new turn to the ideal optimism of his early opinions.

Already before the war his experience of American political life had begun to have a sobering effect on his democratic enthusiasm. "From the age of 21 to 40, (1840–'60)", says he,

I was interested in the political movements of the land, not so much as a participant, but as an observer, and a regular voter at the elections. I think I was conversant with the springs of action, and their workings, not only in New York city and Brooklyn, but understood them in the whole country, as I had made leisurely tours through all the middle States, and partially through the western and southern, and down to New Orleans, in which city I resided for some time. . . . For twenty-five years previous to the outbreak, the controling "Democratic" nominating conventions of our Republic—starting from their primaries in wards or districts, and so expanding to counties, powerful cities, States, and so to the great Presidential nominating conventions—were getting to represent and be composed of more and more putrid and dangerous materials. Let me give a schedule, or list, of one of these representative conventions for a long time before, and inclusive of, that which nominated Buchanan . . . . One of these conventions, from 1840 to '60, exhibited a spectacle such as could never be seen except in our age and in these States. The members who composed it were, seven-eights of them, the meanest kind of bawling and blowing office-holders, office-seekers, pimps, malignants, conspirators, murderers, fancy-men, custom-house clerks, contractors, kept-editors, spaniels well-train'd to carry and fetch, jobbers, infidels, disunionists, terrorists, mail-riflers, slave-catchers, pushers of slavery, creatures of the President, creatures of would-be Presidents, spies, bribers, compromisers, lobbyers, sponges, ruin'd sports, expell'd gamblers, policy-backers, monte-dealers, duellists, carriers of conceal'd weapons, deaf men, pimpled men, scarr'd inside with vile disease, gaudy outside with gold chains made from the people's money and harlots' money twisted together; crawling, serpentine men, the lousy combings and born freedom-sellers of the earth. And whence came they? From back-yards and bar-rooms; from out of the custom-houses, marshals' offices, post-offices, and gambling halls; from the President's house, the jail, the station-house; from unnamed by-places, where devilish disunion was hatch'd at midnight; from political hearses, and from the coffins inside, and from the shrouds inside of the coffins; from the tumors and abscesses of the land; from the skeletons and skulls in the vaults of the federal alms-houses; and from the running sores of the great cities.[21]

Not a very reassuring picture to the lover of democratic government, and certainly not a very massive basis on which to found the conception of a state as an all-embracing comradeship. That Whitman's mind was often filled with bitter misgivings he himself confesses. So deeply was he impressed with the evils which grew rank under the aegis of republican institutions that his faith in democracy began to waver, and he confesses frankly that but for the war, its phenomena, and results so far as they came within his personal observation, *Leaves of Grass*—with its radically democratic *Weltanschauung*—would never have gone beyond the embryonic first editions. The war, of which he was such a profound spectator, settled his doubts. It brought to an issue the all-important question whether the American Union was merely a materialistic concern, was merely a compromise of conflicting elements, or whether, beneath and beyond all those material interests, there existed a pervading sentiment of union; a national conviction which refused to be tampered with; a latent spiritual volcano in the national will, whose force, in abeyance while corrupt politicians disported themselves in the political arena, was to sweep them and their doings into limbo at the very first appearance of real danger. From the very start he felt instinctively that the question at issue was not merely one of political union, but one which concerned the very nature and credentials of democracy.[22] And he sums up the result of the war from his point of view as follows:

I have said somewhere that the three Presidentiads preceding 1861 show'd how the weakness and wickedness of rulers are just as eligible here in America under republican, as in Europe under dynastic influences. But what can I say of that prompt and splendid wrestling with secession slavery, the arch-enemy personified, the instant he unmistakeably show'd his face? The volcanic upheaval of the nation, after that firing on the flag at Charleston, proved for certain something which had previously been in great doubt, and at once substantially settled the question of disunion. In my judgment it will remain as the grandest and most encouraging spectacle yet vouchsafed in any age, old or new, to political progress and democracy. It was not for what came to the surface merely—though that was important—but what it indicated below, which was of eternal importance. Down in the abysms of New World humanity there had formed and hardened a primal hard-pan of national Union will, determin'd and in the majority, refusing to be tamper'd with or argued against, confronting all emergencies, and capable at any time of bursting all surface bonds, and breaking out like an earthquake. It is, indeed, the best lesson of the century, or of America, and it is a mighty privilege to have been part of it. (Two great spectacles, immortal proofs of democracy, unequall'd in all the history of the past, are furnish'd by the secession war—one at the beginning, the other at its close. Those are, the general, voluntary, arm'd upheaval, and the peaceful and harmonious disbanding of the armies in the summer of 1865.) [23]

The issue of the war being of such vital importance to his entire *Weltanschauung,* what wonder that its varying fortunes before the decisive moment came affected him most profoundly. Indeed, it is not certain that the physical collapse which commenced in 1864 and was consummated in 1873 was not due more to the mortal strain to which the vicissitudes of the war subjected his nervous system than to his work in the hospitals. The language in which he refers to the agony he endured while the fate of the Union was hanging in a balance seems to justify this view. Take, for instance, the following two passages:

> Year that trembled and reel'd beneath me!
> Your summer wind was warm enough, yet the air I breathed
> froze me,
> A thick gloom fell through the sunshine and darken'd me,
> Must I change my triumph songs? said I to myself,
> Must I indeed learn to chant the cold dirges of the baffled?
> And sullen hymns of defeat? [24]

And again:

> Short as the span of our national life has been, already have death and downfall crowded close upon us—and will again crowd close, no doubt, even if warded off. Ages to come may never know, but I know, how narrowly during the late secession war—and more than once, and more than twice or thrice—our Nationality, (wherein bound up, as in a ship in a storm, depended, and yet depend, all our best life, all hope, all value,) just grazed, just by a hair escaped destruction. Alas! to think of them! the agony and bloody sweat of certain of those hours! those cruel, sharp, suspended crises! [25]

The doubts and misgivings which he felt so acutely during that period, coupled with the deepening of his emotional nature, resulted in a profounder grasp of the idea of nationality, its limitations and its needs. The vague, though beautiful, conception of an all-embracing comradeship was not sufficiently practical by the light of the experience he had bought so dearly. The more practical question began to suggest itself: how that sentiment of national comradeship could be induced in a hard-headed, money-loving people; and how it could be so strengthened in its universal operative force as to be a sufficient safeguard against the storms whose accumulated violence was now and again to burst with possibly disastrous effect on the commonwealth.

The outlines of Whitman's answer to these questions will be found in the following chapter. All we are here concerned with is the contribution to his development which is directly traceable to the war period. And this may be summed up by saying that while the phenomena of the war supplied him with the material for a deeper probing of the general problem of democracy, they also convinced him that the bulk of the American people was radically sound, and formed no unworthy basis for the high democratic ideal of his aspirations.

I know not how it may have been, or may be, to others—to me the main interest I found, (and still, on recollection find,) in the rank and file of the armies, both sides, and in those specimens amid the hospitals, and even the dead on the field. To me the points illustrating the latent personal character and eligibilities of these States, in the two or three millions of American young and middle-aged men, North and South, embodied in those armies—and especially the one-third or one-fourth of their number, stricken by wounds or disease at some time in the course of the contest—were of more significance even than the political interests involved. (As so much of the race depends on how it faces death, and how it stands personal anguish and sickness. . . .) [26]

6

Period of Applied Spiritualism
(1866-1873)

Factors of Experience

NO SPECIAL events mark the period that elapsed between the end of the war and 1873, when a stroke of paralysis prostrated Whitman. In February 1864 he had an illness which the doctors diagnosed to be malarial fever due to too constant attendance at the hospitals. From the effects of this illness he never quite recovered, although he continued to work as a government clerk at Washington. It undoubtedly diminished his physical vitality, and thus allowed the currents of his being to run more uninterruptedly in the channels of thought and thoughtful meditation. The immense force of passion which he put into the expression of his ideas during the period of naturalism showed itself not only in a daring originality and a poetic momentum—before whose onrush the reader either goes down with admiration or retires with indignation—but also in a certain turbidity, a certain want of clearness. Then, too, the ordinary reader perhaps feels that the kingdom of heaven cannot be taken by storm, that the higher regions of the spiritual world cannot be reached by a Titanic piling of Pelion on Ossa. Judging from his own experience, perhaps, or from the testimony of Holy Writ, or by the light of other authorities, the ordinary reader feels that the "still small voice" of a higher reality cannot be heard mid the din of such world-defiant efforts. When he reads, in "Song of Myself", such lines as these:

Divine am I inside and out, and I make holy whatever I touch or
    am touch'd from,
The scent of these arm-pits aroma finer than prayer,
This head more than churches, bibles, and all the creeds,[1]

he may perhaps recognise that the writer is engaged in a most heroic effort to solve one of the hardest problems of human thought and life; may even go so far as to admit that what the writer says is substantially and profoundly true; but he will not admit that the defiant spirit breathing through those lines becomes a man; he will protest that such was not the spirit of those leaders of our race who extended the sovereignty of light further into the regions of darkness.

But if that candid reader were to read on in *Leaves of Grass* till he came to the poems written during the years comprised within this period of spiritualism, he would notice a marked change, not only in the subjects, but also in their treatment and tone. The change is not sudden; the transition is not abrupt; yet the difference must strike even the most superficial. The years of quarrying in the darker and less frequented ranges of human experience had brought the philosophic mind —aye, and the spiritual mind too.

Besides, sickness with its resulting diminution of the physical force and spirits had begun to temper the noonday glare of the triumphant, dazzling ego; and in the subdued light of life's afternoon new phenomena were displayed. The new tints and shades—mystic vistas, at once indicating and adumbrating the long unfathomable future—were beginning to react on the poet's experience and to colour his thought. His ideas now became clearer; common basis and interdependence became more striking. The explanation and ultimate ground of the seen were being more and more consciously assigned to and discovered in its only true source for us—the unseen.

Towards this result another factor—the exact value of which in Whitman's case I have never been able to determine—was now contributing. Whitman had begun—at what time I don't know [2]—to study German philosophy. Though he never mastered it technically, the influence of the larger ideas and more important results of the Hegelian dialectic is unmistakably perceptible, especially in his later prose. They probably helped to clarify and harmonise his own poetically conceived ideas of the universe.

Before going further, and with a view to forestalling misconceptions and disarming prejudice, let me very briefly explain here in what sense I use the word "spiritualism" as a heading for this and the succeeding chapter. Some readers may be led to suppose from that heading that I am at this stage entering the quagmire of Swedenborgian mysticism; and such I wish to reassure before going further.

The phenomena of the external world disclose to us what is popularly called "matter" and also certain states or affections of that matter. As soon as we begin to reflect about matter and its states, we begin either to discover or to interpolate another class of experiences. We find, for instance, that there must be "forces" accounting for the various conditions in which matter exists, or the changes which we see matter undergoing. Looking still more attentively at the states of matter, we discover another idea besides force; we find that the various states of matter are owing to the inherence of "energy" in matter; and science has gone so far as to establish that this energy is indestructible; once in existence, it never disappears, although it may change from one state to another. Energy is, so to speak, the immortal soul of matter and undergoes all the vicissitudes of transmigration which some systems of religion assigned or assign to the souls of men and animals.

Now, if we try to think of our experience or the states of the supposed matter, we find it impossible to understand or explain them without resorting to these ideas of force and energy. Whether there are really such things as force and energy existing in matter, we do not know. It may be that force, for instance, is the result of our personal life or subjective experience, and no objective reality at all. And yet, so essential is it to our thought that one might as well try to see without eyes or feel without touch as explain his experiences without interpolating the idea of force. Hence, in our reflection upon our experiences of the material world we inevitably fall back upon an apparatus of stereotyped ideas or invisible entities.

Coming next to our subjective experiences and those of the race, we find again certain ideas—indefinite in number, and much more indefinite and variable in meaning than force and energy—permeating, even originating, those experiences. But in the aggregate they are just as essential to those experiences as are force and energy in our experience of matter. Looking at the experience of humanity and ourselves as a whole, we find that there are certain great ideas, or ideal potencies, at the bottom of most of that experience; certain ideal centres of attraction round which most of that experience—at least in its more advanced stages—groups itself. Such are the principal ideas of political and personal freedom; of responsibility; of religion, etc. All the progress and life of the race can be expressed in terms of these and other ideas; and without them it would be impossible to understand the conscious or unconscious trends of individual and collective progress. Hence, in the subjective experience of humanity we find ideas dominating with as absolute sway as force and energy dominate our experience of the material world.

I call these entities ideas; but it must be remembered that in their operation in history and life they exercise the influence of real living agencies. Whether they have objective counterparts, we cannot say; unless we are willing to guess, with Plato and others.

From this it might probably appear that there is very good ground for looking upon the visible world more as the expression of that invisible ideal order than as existing *per se*. And people who do so look upon the visible world would be properly called idealists. But suppose something more is added to this idealism. Suppose that the idealist looks upon the world not merely in the dry light of the intellect, but rather in the suffused glow of the emotional temperament. Suppose, further, that he looks upon this ideal order as somehow in harmony with human needs and destiny, and as pervaded in some sense with unconscious purposiveness—with an immanent necessity which shapes all change and growth towards some end or ends. In that case mere intellectual idealism would become transformed by the elements of emotion and faith into what I call spiritualism.

Spiritualism is therefore the attitude of the mind which, diving below the phenomena of the semblant world, finds an anchor of hope and faith in some underlying reality. And the spiritualist is he to whom belief in the reality of this ideal, invisible order of the universe remains not a mere barren intellectual conviction, but becomes a source of moral, artistic, and spiritual strength.

The Idea of the Whole

Let us now single out one of the ideas just referred to, which have the force and vitality of real entities—the idea of the whole. It has perhaps not yet exercised any great historical influence in the shaping of thought and belief; but I venture to think that it will probably become one of the mightiest intellectual and spiritual forces of the future. Let us for a moment —even at the risk of repetition—look at its growth in Whitman's mind and the dominating influence it came finally to exercise over the rest of his ideas and opinions.

Starting from the dissolving, emotional, flux capacity as the ultimate form of Whitman's personality, we found that a special characteristic of that capacity was its boundless sentient receptivity, or what I also called its universalising extensity. Then it was pointed out how the great complex distinctions of politics, morals, religion, and life were drawn into the vortex of this all-absorptive capacity and there dissolved or disintegrated into their constituent elements. Order became but a means to the great end of social and individual progress; and anarchism, as being another such means, was lifted into a position of co-equality with order. Good became not an end in itself, but a help towards the "progress of souls of men and women along the grand roads of the universe". But evil, being admittedly another such aid to spiritual progress, was rehabilitated and forcibly reconciled to good. The devil was deprived of his separate status and jurisdiction and suddenly—and perhaps not to his entire satisfaction—made a side of the square deific. Finally, death lost his dread throne in the chamber of horrors and became (with birth) the alternative midwife—nurse in the illimitable kingdom of life. Thus, one after another the great distinctions of life and thought were swept away, and equality once more recovered her primeval domain.

But the practical question is: Was this vast dissolving process merely carrying things back to the original state of chaos, or was it starting a tendency towards a greater ideal cosmos? The answer, one way or the other, depends on a certain distinction, and the question how far that distinction was recognised by Whitman. If it was his intention to cause a permanent disturbance of men's practice by sweeping away the fundamental distinctions on which that practice is based, he was certainly an emissary of chaos. But if, by his mergence of the distinctions underlying the practical life of the individual and society, he did not intend to dislocate that practice from its ancient grooves, but merely or chiefly to introduce into men's thought a new point of view, from which that practice would derive greater ethical and spiritual significance, which in return would react beneficially on the practice—if, in other words, he did not wish to change men's ethical practice, but rather to deepen, broaden, and spiritualise the ideal bases and assumptions on which that practice is founded—he may possibly be the herald of a new cosmos.

I think the evidence in support of either of these alternatives is conflicting during the period of naturalism. On the one hand may be quoted such passages as those in which he clearly enunciates that the second alternative is within the scope of his general intention. On the other hand, many passages may be adduced to show that his clear and direct purpose was to upset current ways of life as well as current modes of thought. I conclude, therefore, that up to 1862 Whitman was not clear as to the practical purport and general bearings of his thought. He spoke because necessity was laid on him without having yet clearly realised the probable results of his views if they were to be generally accepted. In other words, although his flux capacity had brought into motion the standing landmarks of human thought and practice; although, therefore, the germinant idea of the whole was clearly operating in the direction of a coordination, an all-embracing harmonisation of the factors in cosmic life, yet that idea had not yet found its true centre in the Ideal.

Now, if one thing is more certain than another, it is that no harmony is possible between the practical results of the world process. The empirical world of first-hand experience presents antimonies and discrepancies which cannot be reconciled except from a point of view that transcends the actual. Like contemporary Europe, the cosmic process works for peace and harmony by keeping up vast armaments of hostile and mutually destructive forces. I cannot find that Whitman had, during the period of naturalism, discovered the point of view from which this conflict of the actual or phenomenal vanishes. But as the merely physical relaxed its hold on him from 1864 onwards, his inner eye began to see more clearly the ideal world, in which alone the coloured rays of empirical existence melt insensibly into the mild radiance of white light; in which alone the confused noises of the actual combine into the full harmony of the ideal, which is for us also the real. In the ideal he found the coign of vantage from which he could feast his inner eye on the panorama of the whole. There, at last, his idea of the whole was consummated.

From the development just recapitulated, it must not be supposed that the idea of the whole was first formulated in the period of spiritualism now under consideration. Under the name of *ensemble* it appears early in the period of naturalism. Take, for instance, the following lines from "Starting from Paumanok":

I will not make poems with reference to parts,
But I will make poems, songs, thoughts, with reference to ensemble,
And I will not sing with reference to a day, but with reference to
  all days,
And I will not make a poem nor the least part of a poem but has
  reference to the soul,
Because having look'd at the objects of the universe, I find there
  is no one nor any particle of one but has reference to the soul.[3]

Not only does this quotation clearly express the idea of ensemble; it also states it to be one of the basic conceptions in *Leaves of Grass,* and further indicates (in the last two lines) the general spiritual significance of the idea. But, as I have already pointed out, Whitman did not yet fully understand the import of this idea.

It is in the remarkable "Song of the Universal" that we first find a clear statement of the deeper significance of the idea.

In this broad earth of ours,
Amid the measureless grossness and the slag,
Enclosed and safe within its central heart,
Nestles the seed perfection.[4]

This is no mere summing up of the phenomenal without distinction or discrimination; no mere undiscriminating panegyric on the cosmic sum total, such as we sometimes find in his earlier work. He had begun to look deeper for the true meaning and bearings of the cosmos; and he had found the tiny but fruitful seed of perfection nestling beneath the imposing but unstable pageant of appearance.

But does Whitman not in the very first stanza of this poem on the universal recede from the standpoint of universality and fall back on that cosmic dualism which he wishes to escape from? If there is this measureless slag on the one hand, and the seed of perfection on the other, the escape from dualism seems illusory. To this Whitman's practical answer (he eschews all metaphysical hair-splitting) is that the seed of perfection is not a separate entity, but immanent in and inseparably identified with the slag. The dualism in thought is not a dualism in reality.

By every life a share or more or less,
None born but it is born, conceal'd or unconceal'd the seed is
    waiting.[5]

And developing this idea of the immanent seed of perfection, the universal energising through and vitalising the abnormal, partial, singular, he says:

Out of the bulk, the morbid and the shallow,
Out of the bad majority, the varied countless frauds of men and
    states,
Electric, antiseptic yet, cleaving, suffusing all,
Only the good is universal.

Over the mountain-growths, disease and sorrow,
An uncaught bird is ever hovering, hovering,
High in the purer, happier air.

From imperfection's murkiest cloud,
Darts always forth one ray of perfect light,
One flash of heaven's glory.

To fashion's, custom's discord,
To the mad Babel-din, the deafening orgies,
Soothing each lull a strain is heard, just heard,
From some far shore the final chorus sounding,

O the blest eyes, the happy hearts,
That see, that know the guiding thread so fine,
Along the mighty labyrinth.[6]

As this idea of the whole is of the greatest importance when applied to the cosmos, let us see how it is presented in Whitman's profound criticism of Carlyle, written in 1881 or 1882:

There is, apart from mere intellect, in the make-up of every superior human identity, (in its moral completeness, considered as *ensemble,* not for that moral alone, but for the whole being, including physique,) a wondrous something that realizes without argument, frequently without what is called education, (though I think it the goal and apex of all education deserving the name)—an intuition of the absolute balance, in time and space, of the whole of this multifarious, mad chaos of fraud, frivolity, haggishness—this revel of fools, and incredible make-believe and general unsettledness, we call *the world;* a soul-sight of that divine clue and unseen thread which holds the whole congeries of things, all history and time, and all events, however trivial, however momentous, like a leash'd dog in the hand of the hunter. Such soul-sight and root-centre for the mind—mere optimism explains only the surface or fringe of it—Carlyle was mostly, perhaps entirely without. He seems instead to have been haunted in the play of his mental action by a spectre, never entirely laid from first to last, . . . the spectre of world-destruction.[7]

It was this "soul-sight of that divine clue", putting the individual *en rapport* with the universe in which he lives, that raised Whitman above the storms and jarring discords of optimism and pessimism, good and evil, right and wrong, which vex the lower ranges of thought. From that higher vantage-ground of insight and faith he could see the vast and harmonious perspective of the moral universe; the different, yet co-operant, forces whose aggregate play was necessary to the maintenance and progress of that universe. It was that soul-sight that filled his mind with a peace which the anomalies of the semblant world could not take away. He was at peace with himself, with the world, with his fellows, with God, with the devil, if one may say so.

It is obvious that we have here the taproot of Whitman's philosophy; the central idea which, springing from the universalising extensity of his primordial personality and slowly cutting its way through the vast overgrowth of his empirical experience, ultimately came to shape and dominate all his other ideas. From that standpoint in the ideal and survey of the whole he could see how the anarchistic tendency reacted on the corpus of stagnant inertia to produce progress and order; how the soul, like the charioteer in the *Phaedrus,* was drawn over the long roads of endless existence by the horses of Good and Evil. And he saw that it was foolish and impious to recognise any philosophy or theology which destroyed the ultimate unity and harmony of all things; which discovered a seam anywhere in the divine garment of existence; which found a gap or hiatus anywhere in the eternally progressive continuity; which recognised the devil's claim to any part of this God's world.

Let us now consider some other results that follow from the idea of the whole.

The idea of the whole brings into prominence the biological element that lies behind ethical distinctions.

The idea of the whole is perhaps the most essential and fundamental idea in art. Whatever is fragmentary or partial is an offense against art and so far an offense against beauty. It is only in the whole, in the completion of proportion and symmetry, in the complete consummation of the relations constituting the whole, that the highest beauty can be displayed.

The idea of the whole is also unseparably connected with life. As life is indivisible, all the phenomena of life form natural units, each being a complete whole. In the unimpeded course of nature, a fraction of a tree, a horse, a man, is a simple impossibility.

On the other hand, moral distinctions are not based on the idea of the whole so much as on the assumption of parts. Goodness is a purely relative term: an act is good only in so far as it contributes towards a certain desirable end; it is bad only in so far as it prevents the attainment of that desirable end. In other words, it is only when a whole is considered as consisting of parts that it can be said that some are good and others are bad according as they do or do not contribute towards the efficiency or desirability of the whole.

Summing up these statements, we see that art largely and life altogether involve the idea of the whole, while ethical distinctions are based on the relations of parts to the whole. The idea of the whole consequently tends to give to beauty and life a certain prominence over good. Leaving beauty aside, and assuming that health or sanity is one of the most essential elements in the conception of life, we may also state this result as follows: the idea of the whole tends towards the substitution of health or sanity for goodness as a moral criterion. But we have already seen that Whitman's thought is pervaded more by biological than ethical ideas of human conduct and relations. This is therefore a strong indication of the extent to which the idea of the whole had—at first perhaps unconsciously—leavened Whitman's thought.

We have just assumed that health or sanity is inherent in life. In fact, all life is in itself healthy; and in so far as it is sickly, it is not life, but decay. Without stopping to notice the feeble and querulous objection of the constitutional pessimist, we may conclude from this most reasonable assumption that the cosmic process, so far as it is a process, an evolution, a life, so far it is also sane and healthy. From this follows an invincible faith in progress—another characteristic of Whitman.

But the most important results of this idea of the whole are the cosmic faith and the idea of God.

When the idea of the cosmic whole as a sane and healthy process takes hold of a mind of great emotional and spiritual capacity, it will become the great attractive and coordinative centre of all its higher ideas. Such was the case with Whitman. And hence the significance of the three following statements; one taken from the 1855 edition of *Leaves of Grass,* the second from "Criticism on Carlyle" (1881 or 1882), and the third from "Democratic Vistas".[8]

Sanity and ensemble characterize the great master; spoilt in one principle, all is spoilt.

The greatest religious and the profoundest philosopher is he who accepts in perfect faith the moral unity and sanity of the creative scheme.

This is put less laconically in "Democratic Vistas":

Standing on this ground [religion]—the last, the highest, only permanent ground—and sternly criticising, from it, all works, whether of the literary, or any art, we have peremptorily to dismiss every pretensive production, however fine its aesthetic or intellectual points, which violates or ignores, or even does not celebrate, the central divine idea of All, suffusing universe, of eternal trains of purpose, in the development, by however slow degrees, of the physical, moral, and spiritual kosmos. I say he has studied, meditated to no profit, whatever may be his mere erudition, who has not absorb'd this simple consciousness and faith.

Thus the idea of the whole, implying the idea of cosmic health and sanity, became the fundamental assumption in Whitman's thought—the one great faith from which he would never recede and in which he saw the most potent factor of future spiritual progress. As he contemplates this idea of the whole, of the universal, and ponders its profound implications, and its possible meaning for future thought and life, it kindles in him the white heat of spiritual passion:

Give me O God to sing that thought,
Give me, give him or her I love this quenchless faith,
In Thy ensemble, whatever else withheld withhold not from us,
Belief in plan of Thee enclosed in Time and Space,
Health, peace, salvation universal.[9]

Summing up the foregoing, we may say that the idea of the cosmic whole, considered not as an assemblage of empirical phenomena, but as an underlying, indivisible, enduring, sane process, became in Whitman's mind the radical foundation of the cosmic faith.

The derivation of the idea of God from the idea of the whole will be found in Chapter 7.

It remains now to trace the moulding influence of this idea of the whole and this cosmic faith on Whitman's conceptions of democracy, of literature, and of religion.

Democracy

As democracy is one of the great *momenta* of *Leaves of Grass,* one of the central themes round which a large number of Leaves naturally group themselves, Whitman's views on the subject can be generally gathered from the Leaves themselves. But during the period now under treatment, Whitman wrote "Democratic Vistas", in which he gave a more-or-less connected account of his views on the nature, functions, and destiny of democracy; and this essay will be the principal authority for this section.

It is certainly remarkable that "Democratic Vistas" has not attracted more attention than has yet been accorded to it; for whether we consider its general picturesqueness and occasional sublimity of style, or whether we consider its searching criticism, its pregnant suggestions, its largeness of conception, or its profound spirit, it would be hard to find any piece of writing on the great subject of democracy of equal importance and fascination. No more striking and suggestive contrast could be imagined than that between "Democratic Vistas" and Carlyle's "Chartism": both belonging to the same great historical epoch, but the one coming from the despairing prophet-critic of the past, the other from the brooding, rapt hierophant of the future. Probably it is the exalted spirituality and large ideas, more than the involved rhetoric, of "Democratic Vistas" which have militated against its general popularity.

In giving an account of the main thoughts of that profound essay, I am obliged, by the difference of our points of view, to diverge somewhat from the lines taken by Whitman. For while his subject was democracy, mine is democracy considered as the joint product of Whitman's personality and experience. The results of both the objective and subjective methods of treatment will be practically identical.

Coming now to Whitman's view of the nature and functions of democracy, we find two main ideas underlying his conception. The first is the idea of a people considered not merely as a summation of individuals, but as itself a great composite individual with certain characteristics and certain laws of development. This I have already referred to in a previous chapter. The second underlying idea is that of society as a process. The connection between the two ideas has just been traced at the beginning of this chapter.

From this conception of a people as a whole, and as a process, follow certain important general corollaries, which must be briefly referred to.

▶ *The essence of society is not institutions,*
stereotyped forms, and governments.

The careful student of Whitman's conception of democracy is not long in discovering from both *Leaves of Grass* and his prose writings that this conception is wanting very largely in the elements of social and political organisation. He does indeed seem to have attached great importance to the Year One, and the Constitution of these States; and occasionally he cites that Constitution as a practical proof of the superiority of the democratic over the "feudal" schemes of government. But from occasional statements and from a general silence on the topic one may fairly conclude that Whitman considered the political side of democracy as among its least suggestive and interesting, if not among its less important, aspects.

One cannot help thinking that this is a flaw in his general view. One need not go further back than the history of Great Britain to see what profound, indeed incalculable, influence political government exercises over the national character and habits and the destiny of a people.

It is not too much to say that the methods of the British constitution have coloured the thoughts, the philosophy, even the religion and idealism of the British people. To this it is no pertinent retort to say that the constitution, philosophy, and religion of this people are all effects of a common cause. For such a statement is as specially misleading as it is generally true. There can be no doubt that the methods of political government in this country, while having, with other forms of national life, a common origin in the national character, have in turn reacted on that character and largely affected those forms. The *constitutional* point of view dominates as significantly the general thought and life of Englishmen as it is absent from the thought and life of Continental peoples. Even revolutions are in England strangely constitutional.

Further: as a people is an organism, the solidarity and organic continuity in political forms and traditions are such that, whether for good or evil, a people's past largely determines its future. Woe to that people over whose past an evil genius has presided! Revolutions may come; the political Ethiopian may be painted white; and the magic words that bring peace and prosperity to other peoples may be inscribed on its banners. In a short time the old genius will reappear; and following in its wake, the dread implacable forces of corrupting political traditions:

$$\sigma\epsilon\iota\nu\alpha\grave{\iota}\ \delta\ddot{\alpha}\mu'\ \ddot{\upsilon}\pi\text{o}\nu\tau\alpha\iota$$
$$\kappa\hat{\eta}\alpha\epsilon\varsigma\ \dot{\alpha}\pi\lambda\acute{\alpha}\kappa\eta\nu\text{o}\iota.\text{[10]}$$

In fact, such is the solidarity of age with age that one is perhaps justified in saying that a people never cuts itself away from its past without committing national suicide.

From this point of view the fatal error of making light of political shortcomings becomes clear. Whitman, and indeed Americans generally, seem to regard with too light a heart the corruption which is blighting political and municipal life in the States. Whitman seems to have looked for the political salvation of the States to the intervention of the "divine average" —the silent American commonalty who at present regard the political corruption with more or less of indifference. No doubt the average citizen is the only "immortal boss"; but no doubt, too, the average citizen very seldom plays the heroic part of a *deus ex machina*. Too often he remains indifferent till indifference becomes a matter not of choice, but necessity—subjective or objective. I do not impugn the fundamental correctness of Whitman's probing of American democracy; but it does seem to me that his constitutional disregard for forms, methods, traditions largely veiled from him the evil heritage which American democracy is bequeathing to coming generations.

His apparent neglect of "forms" was not confined to the constitutional, but extended even to the legal and proprietary bases of American society. While he has the largest and most inspiring conception of the moral and spiritual destinies of democracy, he seems to think that the present relations of state and private ownership, together with a general material comfort among the people,[11] will be a sufficient material basis for that spiritual superstructure. On the other hand, most competent thinkers seem to agree in holding that the changes that democracy will effect in the proprietary structure of society will be not a whit less far-reaching than its probable effect in social and political reorganisation. Then, too, although democratic social evolution seems likely to lead to conditions in which the family as the basis of society will have to pass through the firiest ordeals, yet Whitman seems to have no hesitation in making the family the true organic basis of future democratised society. Indeed, one may say that the student will read Whitman to greatest advantage if he expects to find little or nothing in him on the important subject of forms and institutions—constitutional, municipal, social, legal, proprietary. The program for the future, such as he conceives it, is drawn up on altogether different lines and touches quite other issues.

▶ *Society is an immanent process moulding institutions and governments.*

While we have so far outgrown the inverted mediaeval point of view as to look upon nature as no longer—to use the phrase of Goethe—a mechanical clockwork ticking at the bidding of an external agency; while we have learned to regard nature as in a sense self-sufficient and dominated by an immanent life of its own, we have not yet sufficiently realised the fact that human society, too, is moulded by internal forces, which all spring from the gradually unfolding vitality of the social organism. As Whitman puts it,[12] democracy is younger brother to nature, and is a fact, an indisputable fact of social evolution. No great geniuses have consciously forwarded the movement of democracy; the great plan had not shaped itself in some great "cosmical artist-minds" before it began to be executed. The imperious, mysterious, abysmic forces underlying the organic life of society have done the work. And truly it is a great work. To carp at democracy is therefore ultimately as foolish as to carp at gravitation. All that we are really justified and entitled to do is to recognise it as a fact, as part of the necessity which hedges our conscious life, and to shape our course of action—whether individual or collective—in the wisest manner with reference to that fact.

► *This process consists in the eternally readjusted equilibrium between the individual personality and the social organism.*

The process of historical evolution shows both a synthetic and an analytic tendency. While it consists on the one hand in the gradual intensification, vivification, and organic realisation of the immanent life of the corporate personality, on the other hand it shows a gradual tendency for the unit in the complex organism to emerge, define, and realise itself. From the twilight of the historical dawn we see that unit slowly passing through the ever-narrowing concentric circles of the tribal, gentile, and family groups until finally it has arrived, or is arriving, at the common centre, and thus assumes its true position as the ultimate unit in the social organism. I have already tried—not indeed to define, but—vaguely to indicate my view of this mysterious personality, which is the basis of society. It is the individual, but it is more than that: it is the individual considered as an organism and developing according to its own ineffaceable internal "form" and laws. Whitman indicates his own, less prosaic, conception of the personality in the following passage:

There is, in sanest hours, a consciousness, a thought that rises, independent, lifted out from all else, calm, like the stars, shining eternal. This is the thought of identity—yours for you, whoever you are, as mine for me. Miracle of miracles, beyond statement, most spiritual and vaguest of earth's dreams, yet hardest basic fact, and only entrance to all facts. In such devout hours, in the midst of the significant wonders of heaven and earth, (significant only because of the Me in the centre,) creeds, conventions, fall away and become of no account before the simple idea. Under the luminousness of real vision, it alone takes possession, takes value. Like the shadowy dwarf in the fable, once liberated and look'd upon, it expands over the whole earth, and spreads to the roof of heaven.

The quality of BEING, in the object's self, according to its own central idea and purpose; and of growing therefrom and thereto—not criticism by other standards, and adjustments thereto—is the lesson of Nature.[13]

How to formulate the true relation of this individual to the corporate personality must perhaps always remain an insoluble problem, theoretically. Only the consummated history of the race can form the witness whose testimony can be credited in a matter of such unfathomable meaning and intricacy. From one point of view the corporate personality seems to be the aggregate of all the individual personalities; from another, subtler point of view, the individual personality seems to be nothing but the corporate personality realising itself in the individual. If we take the latter point of view, we can sum up history by saying that it has so far been the unfolding, defining, and identifying of the infant individual personality from the maternal corporate personality. This point of view brings out clearly the vital ties that bind the individual to society. The stamp of society is indelibly impressed on his inmost personality, and the free movement which he requires for his own development will be more or less in harmony with the larger movement of society. From this standpoint individual liberty comes to mean life according to the laws and restraints of existence. And this is the definition which Whitman arrives at, though probably by a different train of reasoning. After saying that liberty means being free from the trammels of creed, fashion, party, vice, he goes on thus:

Strange as it may seem, we only attain to freedom by a knowledge of, and implicit obedience to, Law. Great—unspeakably great—is the Will! the free Soul of man! At its greatest, understanding and obeying the laws, it can then, and then only, maintain true liberty. For there is to the highest, that law as absolute as any—more absolute than any—the Law of Liberty. The shallow, as intimated, consider liberty a release from all law, from every constraint. The wise see in it, on the contrary, the potent Law of Laws, namely, the fusion and combination of the conscious will, or partial individual law, with the universal, eternal, unconscious ones, which run through all Time, pervade history, prove immortality, give moral purpose to the entire objective world, and the last dignity to human life.[14]

But this theoretical definition fails within certain narrow practical limits, which vary with individual cases. For as the historical process does differentiate the individual from the corporate personality, it is obvious that there is a certain small difference between their forms and laws. And in the inherent tendency of both forms to hold their own and push forward their own evolution and realisation, a certain amount of stress and strain arises between the individual and the corporate personality. If perfect harmony were to prevail between the two personalities, there would not be this stress, nor would there be the resultant process or movement of historical evolution. In other words, the perfect assimilation of the individual and the corporate personalities would produce a deadlock in human progress and mark the entry of humanity upon the stage of Nirvana. But so long as there is a certain amount of difference between the forms, laws, and requirements of the two kinds of personality, so long there will be a resultant stress between them; so long, too, there will be endless attempts at readjustment; and so long the evolution of humanity will continue.

▶ *Democracy is that form of society in which the tendency is to adjust this equilibrium most favourably to the individual personality.*

From what has been said just now, it appears that the historical process strengthens both the individual and the corporate personality: both gain more and more of self-consciousness as the process continues; while self-consciousness in turn marshals the forces and factors of life according to certain defined ends and thus stops their random battling and wasteful self-destruction. Especially is this the case with the state or corporate personality. There is no subject of more fascinating interest than studying the gradual focussing of the scattered, feeble rays of the common good and interest from their condition of primeval diffuseness to the present, all-powerful beam of central authority. And the process of concentration and centralisation continues apace. The tides of social legislation, socialism, of collectivism, which are perceptibly heaving the bosom of European society show that the State is going to hold its own, whatever betide. Now, as this augmenting of the forces at the disposal of the State appears inevitable—an inherent attribute of modern and future social organisation—the question arises whether that tendency will not lead to the suppression of the individual, towards the minification of the difference between the respective forms of the individual and the corporate personality; and, as an inevitable consequence, to the sterilisation or exhaustion both of the individual and the State.

The question points to a real danger; perhaps the most formidable rock ahead of the fair ship of Western civilisation. The social forces may gradually undermine the tendency to individual variation, until every citizen will ultimately be a flawless, dull, tax-paying, patent individual, neither above nor below the official standard. Thinkers are beginning to give their attention to the subject. But long before the appearance of these thinkers, the self-regulating process of social evolution had begun to introduce some checks, most important and far-reaching, among which is democracy. It is removing slowly, but unceasingly, the iron swaddling-clothes in which the infancy of the individual personality was nourished. The artificial gradations of society under the systems of caste and feudalism are slowly being levelled away. The handicaps which fettered the race of the individual personality are gradually being removed. While ancient and mediaeval society was obliged to make up for the weakness of the State by tightening the social, economic, and ecclesiastical bonds which restrain the egoistic, radical individual and determined his position in the social system, the shifting of the centre of gravity in the modern body politic to the central authority renders most of those bonds obsolete. Salvation for the future lies only in the maximum amount of individual free play that is consistent with the general public good. But let me quote Whitman's own suggestive and impressive language on this point:

For after the rest is said—after the many time-honour'd and really true things for subordination, experience, rights of property, etc., have been listen'd to and acquiesced in—after the valuable and well-settled statement of our duties and relations in society is thoroughly conn'd over and exhausted—it remains to bring forward and modify everything else with the idea of that Something a man is, (last precious consolation of the drudging poor,) standing apart from all else, divine in his own right, and a woman in hers, sole and untouchable by any canons of authority, or any rule derived from precedent, state-safety, the acts of legislatures, or even from what is called religion, modesty, or art. The radiation of this truth is the key of the most significant doings of our immediately preceding three centuries, and has been the political genesis and life of America. Advancing visibly, it still more advances invisibly. Underneath the fluctuations of the expressions of society, as well as the movements of the politics of the leading nations of the world, we see steadily pressing ahead and strengthening itself, even in the midst of immense tendencies toward aggregation, this image of completeness in separatism, of individual personal dignity, of a single person, either male or female, characterized in the main, not from extrinsic acquirements or position, but in the pride of himself or herself alone; and, as an eventual conclusion and summing-up, (or else the entire scheme of things is aimless, a cheat, a crash,) the simple idea that the last, best dependence is to be on humanity itself, and its own inherent, normal, full-grown qualities, without any superstitious support whatever. This idea of perfect individualism it is indeed that tinges and gives character to the idea of the aggregate. For it is mainly or altogether to serve independent separatism that we favor a strong generalization, consolidation.

The purpose of democracy—supplanting old belief in the necessary absoluteness of establish'd dynastic rulership, temporal, ecclesiastical, and scholastic, as furnishing the only security against chaos, crime, and ignorance—is, through many transmigrations, and amid endless ridicules, arguments, and ostensible failures, to illustrate, at all hazards, this doctrine or theory that man, properly train'd in sanest, highest freedom, may and must become a law, and series of laws, unto himself, surrounding and providing for, not only his own personal control, but all his relations to other individuals, and to the State; and that, while other theories, as in the past histories of nations, have proved wise enough, and indispensable perhaps for their conditions, *this,* as matters now stand in our civilized world, is the only scheme worth working from, as warranting results like those of Nature's laws, reliable, when once establish'd, to carry on themselves.[15]

▶ *The mission of democracy is to reduce the exercise of central authority by teaching the people voluntary self-government.*

According to Whitman, we have as yet seen but the beginnings of democracy. Democracy as a form of government, as a distribution of votes, we have learned to know already. We have still to make the acquaintance of democracy as a social, moral, and spiritual principle leavening the vast lump of organised society in all its branches and divisions. We have seen Demos ascend a throne and assume an authority such as no oriental or feudal despot ever dreamed of. That the change in dynasty means also a change in measures and general activity, we have still largely to learn. The supreme function of future democratic government will be—after removing the artificial barriers that thwart the free development of the individual—to surround the individual with the conditions that shall call forth, stimulate, and encourage his natural growth, and train him in habits of self-reliance and self-government instead of dwarfing him under the incubus of its octopus bureaucracy. In criticising Carlyle's views of democracy, Whitman says:

. . . the promise, nay certainty of the democratic principle, to each and every State of the current world, not so much of helping it to perfect legislators and executives, but as the only effectual method for surely, however slowly, training people on a large scale toward voluntarily ruling and managing themselves (the ultimate aim of political and all other development)—to gradually reduce the fact of *governing* to its minimum, and to subject all its staffs and their

doings to the telescopes and microscopes of committees and parties
—the greatest of all to afford (not stagnation and obedient content
which went well enough with the feudalism and ecclesiasticism of
the antique and medieval world, but) a vast and sane and recurrent
ebb and tide action for those floods of the great deep that have
henceforth palpably burst forever their old bounds—seem never to
have enter'd Carlyle's thought.[16]

Discarding both *laissez-faire* and repression, future democratic government must make the culture of the personality the
cardinal feature of its legislative and administrative activity.

We believe the ulterior object of political and all other government . . . to be among the rest, not merely to rule, to repress
disorder, etc., but to develop, to open up to cultivation, to encourage the possibilities of all beneficent and manly outcroppage,
and of that aspiration for independence, and the pride and self-
respect latent in all characters. (Or if there be exceptions, we cannot, fixing our eyes on them alone, make theirs the rule for all.)

I say the mission of government, henceforth, in all civilized lands,
is not repression alone, and not authority alone, not even of law,
nor by that favorite standard of the eminent writer, the rule of the
best men—the born heroes and captains of the race, (as if such ever,
or at one time out of a hundred, get into the big places, elective or
dynastic)—but higher than the highest arbitrary rule, to train com-
munities through all their grades, beginning with individuals and
ending there again, to rule themselves. What Christ appear'd for in
the moral-spiritual field for human-kind, namely, that in respect to
the absolute soul, there is in the possession of such by each single
individual, something so transcendent, so incapable of gradations,
(like life,) that, to that extent, it places all beings on a common
level, utterly regardless of the distinctions of intellect, virtue, sta-
tion, or any height or lowliness whatever—is tallied in like manner,
in this other field, by democracy's rule that men, the nation, as a
common aggregate of living identities, affording in each a separate
and complete subject for freedom, worldly thrift and happiness,
and for a fair chance for growth, and for protection in citizenship,
etc., must, to the political extent of the suffrage or vote, if no
further, be placed, in each and in the whole, on one broad, primary,
universal, common platform.[17]

148

▶ *The continuance of the social process can alone insure the health and safety of democracy.*

Carlyle, although he carefully protested that he had no Morrison's Pill to be administered to the ailing democracy of his day, yet seemed to have a lurking suspicion that there was somewhere such a panacea, as he was continually blaming the politicians for not producing it. But as Whitman points out with perfect correctness from his point of view, the health of society is the result of the immanent process in the social whole; no remedy *ab extra* can effect any radical cure while this process is clogged or otherwise abnormally affected. As a proof of this, it may be pointed out that no people whose moral and social life has once become deeply affected with disease has ever recovered from the consequences. From this point of view Carlyle's "Great Men" theory shrinks to its proper dimensions. History certainly shows that there is no "exclusive curative power in first-class men".

▶ *The evils of democratic government serve to keep up the social process, and thus ultimately conduce towards the health and purity of democracy.*

Because Whitman's cosmic faith, together with his own unrivalled experience, inspires him with hope and trust in the future of humanity, it must not be supposed that therefore he is uncritical in his estimate of the people or of popular government. So far from that being the case, I have nowhere in literature come across such a searching diagnosis of democracy as is to be found in Whitman's works as a whole. His criticism is all the more valuable and penetrating because it is free from all animus. Sometimes he speaks in sorrow; sometimes, again, his words hear traces of the unrecorded struggles that he must have passed through in regard to this subject. But there is not a trace of poison or bitterness; so serene is his trust in the destiny that is guiding our race. That he had no illusions in regard to the evil which is not only in men but also in nations, is amply attested by the following passage:

Meantime, general humanity . . . has always, in every department, been full of perverse maleficence, and is so yet. In downcast hours the soul thinks it always will be—but soon recovers from such sickly moods. I myself see clearly enough the crude, defective streaks in all the strata of the common people; the specimens and vast collections of the ignorant, the credulous, the unfit and uncouth, the incapable, and the very low and poor.[18]

Far from identifying the true principles of democracy with the "money-worshipping, Jesus-and-Judas equalizing suffrage-sovereignty echoes of current America", he was perfectly aware that a "factid gas-bag much of modern radicalism is". Pictures —apparently very faithful, certainly very life-like—of the practical working of democracy in America abound in his writings —pictures far more damaging to the "cause" than any the book-reading Carlyle could have produced. What then? Did this profoundly disillusioning experience shatter his faith in democracy? If it had done so, he would not be the hierophant of the cosmic faith, the ardent lover of the universe, but a mere bellowing optimist. It was because he had probed deeper than the disease, even to the very life on which the disease was preying, that he could preserve his "crown of spiritual manhood", could retain his transcedent faith in humanity. His depth and range of vision, his grasp of the idea of the whole, enabled him to take the true measure of these discouraging phenomena; he assigned to them their true position in the perspective of the whole. He was able to assign to them their true function in sustaining and even stimulating that cosmic process which is the very life of democracy. Thus, he says:

The eager and often inconsiderate appeals of reformers and revolutionists are indispensable, to counterbalance the inertness and fossilism making so large a part of human institutions. The latter will always take care of themselves—the danger being that they rapidly tend to ossify us. The former is to be treated with indulgence, and even with respect. As circulation to air, so is agitation and a plentiful degree of speculative license to political and moral sanity. Indirectly, but surely, goodness, virtue, law, (of the very best,) follow freedom. These, to democracy, are what the keep is to the ship, or saltness to the ocean.[19]

From which, as well as from any other passages, it is clear that Whitman looked upon anarchism, revolutionary claptrap, and demagogism as far more beneficial than detrimental in their effects on the democracy. They serve to counteract the soporfic effect on Demos of the cry, "Peace! Peace!" when there ought to be no peace.

Besides, the struggles in the spacious arenas of democracy are a fit training for the indispensable gymnasts of political liberty and progress.

Political democracy, as it exists and practically works in America, with all its threatening evils, supplies a training-school for making first-class men. It is life's gymnasium, not of good only, but of all. We try often, though we fall back often. A brave delight, fit for freedom's athletes, fills these arenas, and fully satisfies, out of the action in them, irrespective of success. Whatever we do not attain, we at any rate attain the experiences of the fight, the hardening of the strong campaign, and throb with currents of attempt at least. Time is ample. Let the victors come after us. Not for nothing does evil play its part among us. Judging, from the main portions of the history of the world, so far, justice is always in jeopardy, peace walks amid hourly pitfalls, and of slavery, misery, meanness, the craft of tyrants, and the credulity of the populace, in some of their protean forms, no voice can at any time say, They are not. The clouds break a little, and the sun shines out—but soon and certain the lowering darkness falls again, as if to last forever. Yet is there an immortal courage and prophecy in every sane soul that cannot, must not, under any circumstances, capitulate. *Vive,* the attack— the perennial assault! *Vive,* the popular cause—the spirit that audaciously aims—the never-abandon'd efforts, pursued the same amid opposing proofs and precedents.[20]

Further, while the evils of democracy serve their needed purpose, they are themselves evanescent so long as the body politic continues healthy at bottom. As the "cosmical antiseptic virtue" of nature continually digests morbific matter into elements of health—often even into nutriment for highest use and life—so, too, the subtle chemistry in the life-process of a normal democracy continually reorganises its waste-products according to its own requirements. So long as the harmonising life of the whole continues its process, so long it will eliminate or disorganise whatever is alien to it.

Lastly, behind log-rolling, caucus, corruption in all its hideous forms, stands the average citizen, "the only immortal owner and boss", and the final dictator in the national crises. The official corruption of America is a "sad, serious, deep truth":

Yet there are other, still deeper, amply confronting, dominating truths. Over those politicians and great and little rings, and over all their insolence and wiles, and over the powerfulest parties looms a power, too sluggish maybe, but ever holding decisions and decrees in hand, ready, with stern process, to execute them as soon as plainly needed—and at times, indeed, summarily crushing to atoms the mightiest parties, even in the hour of their pride.[21]

The Literature of Democracy

But it is possible, nay necessary, to rise to higher ground. Democracy is not only a form of government, and the only form of government possible for us at the present stage of historical evolution; it is more. Large as looms its governmental or political foreground, the moral and spiritual background—with its shadowy width of range and its far-stretching vistas—is far more significant still. Not till democracy shall have turned the wastes, the long patches of desolation, the low levels of malarial fertility which disfigure the commonalty of humanity, into a garden covered with the "manly outcroppage" of a higher personalism, and pervaded with the aroma of a larger and saner spiritual culture than has yet been known—not till then shall it have its fruition, or realise the promise of its dawn. The governmental institution of democracy we know already. We have still to see the inauguration of the Institution of Literature, to whose guard and guidance are to be committed the ideal and spiritual destinies of the democracy.

But has democracy not the spoils of all past literature at its disposal? What need is there of a new literature? Whitman answers that the arrival of democracy does not only mean the triumph of new forms of government over feudal institutions; it means the victory of larger ideas of human society and destiny, and must necessarily bring with it the expression of those ideas in their own appropriate forms. Every new civilisation necessarily brings with it a new literature; and democracy is not likely to be the one exception:

Democracy has been hurried on through time by measureless tides and winds, resistless as the revolution of the globe, and as far-reaching and rapid. But in the highest walks of art it has not yet a single representative worthy of it anywhere upon the earth. . . . Entirely different and hitherto unknown classes of men, being authoritatively called for in imaginative literature, will certainly appear.[22]

Democracy, on its ideal side, means faith in humanity; or, more accurately, faith in the sanity of the cosmic life-process permeating the people as a whole. Now how far does this cosmic faith pervade the literatures of antiquity and of feudalism?

With the exception perhaps of the Bible, the literature of the past is fractional and select, appealing to the learned, the specially trained. The literature of the future must be universal, appealing to common, average humanity. Poetry, for instance, has too long been sectional, exclusive, petty, shrinking from the average, the universal, the democratic. While the conceptions and cosmic perspective of science on the one hand and German philosophy on the other have revolutionised our ideas of the universe, and vastly extended their scope, contemporary literature still continues largely on the petty lines of antiquated thought. "Poems of myths, fictions, feudalism, conquest, caste, dynastic wars, and splendid exceptional characters and affairs"[23] have characterised the literature of the Old World. We want a literature and poems consistent with science and reality, and appealing to the average or universal citizenship instead of to the coterie or the learned. Democracy wants a literature whose underlying impetus shall be the cosmic spirit.

From another point of view the need of a democratic literature becomes still more clear and imperative. At bottom, feudalism was a very poor, bloody, ghastly affair, essentially brutalising and morally degrading to the human character. And yet feudalism illustrates the truth of the divine saying, "Man shall not live by bread alone". Instead of materialising and sterilising the mediaeval character, it called forth two institutions which guarded and developed its spiritual interests. It was the mediaeval church and mediaeval literature which not only gave to feudal institutions their place in the mediaeval heart, but also largely tempered their essential ferocity and harshness, and invested them with an ideal atmosphere which fascinates even to this day.

Democracy runs the same danger of materialism and brutalism. In an industrial society the causes may be different, but the real danger is the same, if not greater, because more subtle. The rapid upheaval of industrial democracy has resulted in a dislocation of the various factors of progress. While the material advance has been of unprecedented magnitude, the moral and spiritual factors have, as it were, lagged behind. As a result, we have all over Christendom, but especially in America, a passion for money-making, a greed for earthly things, a downright, frank materialism such as the world has probably never seen before. But the modern world is no less under the divine dispensation than the mediaeval; and if something of highest use and beauty and attraction could be made of the institutions of a semi-barbarous militarism, is it unreasonable to suppose that democracy will not, on its own vaster scale, achieve a result at least equally striking? In the church as it exists today, Whitman had very little hope. He therefore naturally turned to the unincorporated institution of literature as the greatest cementing and spiritualising factor in future democratic evolution. It must endear to the affections of the people the institutions of democracy. Greed, oppression, and self-seeking it must confront with the loftier and sterner ideals of a people whose very life and character are rooted in the spiritual world. Not only must it bind the people together with the strong ties of mutual goodwill, of an all-embracing comradeship; but over the world of working reality it must span the blue heaven of the ideal. It must link the seen with the unseen; the real with the ideal; the temporal with the eternal.

Now compare this great ideal with the actual achievements of contemporary writers! How deeply dissatisfied Whitman was with contemporary literature (especially American) appears from his burning words in "Democratic Vistas". For current American journalism he could find no better analogy than "those spreading, undulating masses of squid, in certain regions of the sea, through which the whale swimming, with head half out, feeds". And he characterises the general literature of today as follows:

Today, in books, in the rivalry of writers, especially novelists, success, (so-call'd,) is to him or her who strikes the mean flat average, the sensational appetite for stimulus, incident, persiflage, etc., and depicts, to the common calibre, sensual, exterior life. To such, or the luckiest of them, as we see, the audiences are limitless and profitable; but they cease presently. While this day, or any day, to workmen portraying interior or spiritual life, the audiences were limited, and often laggard—but they last forever.

. . . .

What is the reason our time, our lands, that we see no fresh local courage, sanity, of our own—the Mississippi, stalwart Western men, real mental and physical facts, Southerners, etc., in the body of our literature? especially the poetic part of it. But always, instead, a parcel of dandies and ennuyees, dapper little gentlemen from abroad, who flood us with their thin sentiments of parlors, parasols, piano-songs, tinkling rhymes, the five-hundredth importation —or whimpering and crying about something, chasing one aborted conceit after another, and forever occupied in dyspeptic amours with dyspeptic women.[24]

To make the puny measure of contemporary literature even more contemptible, he immediately prefaces this characterisation with a sketch of the great monuments and creators of past literature in a passage of classic Whitmanese:

For us, along the great highways of time, those monuments stand —those forms of majesty and beauty. For us those beacons burn through all the nights. Unknown Egyptians, graving hieroglyphs; Hindus, with hymn and apothegm and endless epic; Hebrew prophet, with spirituality, as in flashes of lightning, conscience like red-hot iron, plaintive songs and screams of vengeance for tryannies and enslavements; Christ, with bent head, brooding love and peace, like a dove; Greek, creating eternal shapes of physical and aesthetic proportion; Roman, lord of satire, the sword, and the codex;—of the figures, some far-off and veil'd, others nearer and visible; Dante, stalking with lean form, nothing but fibre, not a grain of superfluous flesh; Angelo, and the great painters, architects, musicians; rich Shakspere, luxuriant as the sun, artist and singer of feudalism in its sunset, with all the gorgeous colors, owner thereof, and using them at will; and so to such as German Kant and Hegel, where they, though near us, leaping over the ages, sit again, impassive, imperturbable, like the Egyptian gods. Of these and the like of these, is it too much, indeed, to return to our favorite figure, and view them as orbs and systems of orbs, moving in free paths in the spaces of that other heaven, the cosmic intellect, the soul?

Ye powerful and resplendent ones! ye were, in your atmospheres, grown not for America, but rather for her foes, the feudal and the old—while our genius is democratic and modern. Yet could ye, indeed, but breathe your breath of life into our New World's nostrils—not to enslave us, as now, but, for our needs, to breed a spirit like your own—perhaps, (dare we say it?) to dominate, even destroy, what you yourselves have left! On your plane, and no less, but even higher and wider, must we mete and measure for today and here. I demand races of orbic bards, with unconditional uncompromising sway. Come forth, sweet democratic despots of the west! [25]

So far from having a literature commensurate with the more spacious and advanced civilisation of today, we even fall ridiculously below the level of the past.

But let us look more closely at Whitman's ideas on the future literature of democracy. On this subject, too, the idea of the whole, with its main corollary, the cosmic faith, has moulded his thoughts. The cosmic spirit and the cosmic faith must become the "underlying impetus of all first-class songs". From this the main characteristics of the future literature are easily deducible.

▶ *Suggestiveness, more than technical perfection, will characterise future literature.*

Not so much the actual foreground—important though that be—as the ideal background will differentiate future literary paintings from the perfect models of the past. Their main feature will be their environing spirit, their atmosphere—wide, serene, full of spiritual suggestion, and appealing to the untellable aspirations of the soul. Whitman quotes a passage in which Sainte-Beuve brings out this difference by a few masterly strokes.

"Formerly, during the period term'd classic," says Sainte-Beuve, "when literature was govern'd by recognized rules, he was consider'd the best poet who had composed the most perfect work, the most beautiful poem, the most intelligible, the most agreeable to read, the most complete in every respect,—the Æneid, the Gerusalemme, a fine tragedy. Today, something else is wanted. For us the greatest poet is he who in his works most stimulates the reader's imagination and reflection, who excites him the most himself to poetize. The greatest poet is not he who has done the best; it is he who suggests the most; he, not all of whose meaning is at first obvious, and who leaves you much to desire, to explain, to study, much to complete in your turn." [26]

It is evident that Whitman felt from the start that suggestion, more than form, is to be the main feature of the future poetry, and this feeling had undoubtedly a large influence in determining the shape of *Leaves of Grass*. Thus, in a poem that appeared in the first edition of *Leaves of Grass* already, he says:

Who learns my lesson complete?
Boor, journeyman, apprentice, churchman and atheist,
The stupid and the wise thinker, parents and offspring, merchant,
    clerk, porter and customer,
Editor, author, artist, and schoolboy—draw nigh and commence;

It is no lesson—it lets down the bars to a good lesson,
And that to another, and every one to another still.[27]

Thus the pervading and determining quality of suggestiveness in future literature will make great demands on the individual reader; for it is only in his thoughtful understanding
and cooperative mental effort that the spirit of suggestion can
bear fruit. Thus future literature will, by its mental gymnastic,
train and exercise more than amuse. It will thus contribute
towards the currents of personality.

Books are to be call'd for, and supplied, on the assumption that
the process of reading is not a half-sleep but, in highest sense, an
exercise, a gymnast's struggle; that the reader is to do something for
himself, must be on the alert, must himself or herself construct
indeed the poem, argument, history, metaphysical essay—the text
furnishing the hints, the clue, the start or frame-work. Not the
book needs so much to be the complete thing; but the reader of the
book does. That were to make a nation of supple and athletic
minds, well-train'd, intuitive, used to depend on themselves and
not on a few coteries of writers.[28]

▶ *The cosmic faith will express joy in literature.*

From the cosmic faith, involving the frank acceptance of the
universe as a sane and healthy process, which has helped human
progress so far, and will help it still much further, follows the
spirit of hope, content, gratitude, and joy, which is to pervade
future literature. The idea, still more the practice, of praise
and whole-hearted gratitude has almost disappeared from literature. A main feature of Hebrew song, and still perhaps the most
highly cherished part of church services, it has as good as disappeared from secular literature. This should not be so. Even in
society nothing so rounds off the character with grace and sweetness and attractive beauty as content and gratitude. How much
more should this be the case in the harmonious relation of the
personality to that cosmic power of which it is the manifestation
in the individual! Before literature again learns to raise the
song of hope and joy, before it again mingles with the painful
cry of deathless aspiration the sweeter and softer echoes of praise

and gratitude, it will not play the part in spiritual culture which it seems destined to play. More than any other factor in social life, the joyous and grateful frame of mind, springing from an invincible faith in the power that guides our temporal no less than our spiritual destinies, and finding once more great poetic expression as it did in the infancy of our race, is capable of reducing the friction and softening the asperities of social existence and strengthening the pervading force of loving human comradeship by rooting it in the divine. Until democratic literature reechoes with the emotional and spiritual enforcement and accompaniments which our experience for the last nineteen centuries alone can give, that cry of goodwill which once heralded the dawn of a higher civilisation for our race, it will neither have learned its true spirit nor found its true expression.

Whitman notes the difference of effect produced by outdoor nature on the one hand and the overwhelming mass of poetic works on the other. While nature has a "freeing, dilating, joyous" influence, general literature "exerts a certain constipating, repressing, indoor, and artificial influence". Future literature, to be healthy and natural, must assimilate itself to outdoor nature. In a later passage he declares:

I say the profoundest service that poems or any other writings can do for their reader is not merely to satisfy the intellect, or supply something polish'd and interesting, nor even to depict great passions, or persons or events, but to fill him with vigorous and clean manliness, religiousness, and give him *good heart* as a radical possession and habit.[29]

How consistently he put his own ideas into practice is evidenced by the spirit of joy and content which not only finds expression in particular poems, but also pervades *Leaves of Grass* as a whole. Even death received its sublime hymn of thanks, as we have seen.

▶ *The culture of the personality must become the supreme object of future democratic literature.*

"In the centre of all and object of all stands the Human Being, towards whose heroic and spiritual evolution poems and everything, directly or indirectly tend".[30] While the State can do much, both negatively and positively, for the culture of the personality, literature can do far more. The future democratic literatus must make the "building-up of the masses by building up grand individuals his shibboleth".

Confronted with the tremendous needs of contemporary democracy, with the need among others of counteracting the tendency to personal uniformity already referred to, the literature of the past, still more that of the present, becomes unsatisfactory.

The great poems, Shakspere included, are poisonous to the idea of the pride and dignity of the common people, the life-blood of the democracy. The models of our literature, as we get it from other lands, ultramarine, have had their birth in courts, and bask'd and grown in castle sunshine; all smells of princes' favors. Of workers of a certain sort, we have, indeed, plenty, contributing after their kind; many elegant, many learn'd, all complacent. But touch'd by the national test, or tried by the standards of democratic personality, they wither to ashes. I say I have not seen a single writer, artist, lecturer, or what not, that has confronted the voiceless, but ever erect and active, pervading, underlying will and typic aspirations of the land, in a spirit kindred to itself. Do you call those genteel little creatures American poets? Do you term that perpetual, pistareen, paste-pot work, American art, American drama, taste, verse? I think I hear, echoed as from some mountain-top afar in the west, the scornful laugh of the Genius of these States.[31]

But besides the trend towards levelling and consequent uniformity inherent in the modern tendencies, another and more apparent danger to personality lurks in the current modes of education. The superficial intellectual culture of our day—the Procrustes bed on which society applies its universal standard to the measurement of every member, the Moloch fire through which civilisation is now passing her children—is sapping the very basis of society in the personality, and might be fatal, were it not destined to be short-lived. "To prune, gather, trim, conform, and ever cram and stuff, in the pressure of our days".

As now taught, accepted and carried out, are not the processes of culture rapidly creating a class of supercilious infidels, who believe in nothing? Shall a man lose himself in countless masses of adjustments, and be so shaped with reference to this, that, and the other, that the simply good and healthy and brave parts of him are reduced and clipp'd away, like the bordering of box in a garden? You can cultivate corn and roses and orchards—but who shall cultivate the mountain peaks, the ocean, and the tumbling gorgeousness of the clouds? Lastly—is the readily-given reply that culture only seeks to help, systematize, and put in attitude, the elements of fertility and power, a conclusive reply? [32]

This sort of culture is directly opposed to the central law of our personality—growth, not from without, but from within, according to its primordial forces.

The quality of BEING, in the object's self, according to its own central idea and purpose, and of growing therefrom and thereto—not criticisms by other standards, and adjustments thereto—is the lesson of Nature. True, the full man wisely gathers, culls, absorbs; but if, engaged disproportionately in that, he slights or overlays the precious idiocracy and special nativity and intention that he is, the man's self, the main thing, is a failure, however wide his general cultivation. Thus, in our times, refinement and delicatesse are not only attended to sufficiently, but threaten to eat us up, like a cancer. Already, the democratic genius watches, ill-pleased, these tendencies. Provision for a little healthy rudeness, savage virtue, justification of what one has in one's self, whatever it is, is demanded. Negative qualities, even deficiencies, would be a relief. Singleness and normal simplicity and separation, amid this more and more complex, more and more artificialized state of society—how pensively we yearn for them! how we would welcome their return! [33]

No wonder that Whitman suggests a new "science as it were of healthy, average personalism, on original-universal grounds, the object of which should be to raise up and supply through the States a copious race of superb American men and women, cheerful, religious, ahead of any yet known".[34]

But above all he calls for a new literature, whose intensity shall be commensurate with its range; whose scope shall be the entire cosmos as interpreted by the great ideas of science; whose depth shall be measured by the aboriginal passion for personal realisation, for the emotional and spiritual evolution of the personality, in each individual. When literature thus begins to discharge its true functions in future society, the whole will cease to overwhelm, will no longer crush the human spirit to the low level of materialised existence. The idea of the whole will become the spiritual support of each part, and the realisation of the individual will keep pace with the expanding idea of the whole. Following and developing the words of Christ, the new literature must make clear that the idea of the whole—with its vast collective movements and overwhelming aggregations—be not the death-knell of the personality, but rather a call to a deeper life; the object of its advent must be that "men have life and have it more abundantly". The measure of the greatness and the success of the new literature will be the extent to which it will infuse this new life into the individual and sow broadcast over the democracy the seeds of an endlessly germinating personality. In the vaster harvest of that future literature of personality, the idea of the whole and democracy will have their true fruition.

► *Great ideas form the lifeblood of the democracy.*

It will be the function of future literature to expound, and realise, and render practically operative, these ideas.

The materialistic tendencies of contemporary civilisation, with all its awful developments, impressed Whitman very profoundly. "History is long, long, long, says he":

Shift and turn the combinations of the statement as we may, the problem of the future of America is in certain respects as dark as it is vast. Pride, competition, segregation, vicious wilfulness, and licence beyond example, brood already upon us. Unwieldy and immense, who shall hold in behemoth? who bridle leviathan? Flaunt it as we choose, athwart and over the roads of our progress loom huge uncertainty, and dreadful, threatening gloom. It is useless to deny it: Democracy grows rankly up the thickest, most noxious, deadliest plants and fruits of all—brings worse and worse invaders—brings newer, larger, stronger, keener compensations and compellers.[35]

Against this materialism and the poison it subtly distils, not only into the individual character, but the whole body politic; against its hideous outgrowths and cancerous desolation and depletion of spiritual humanity, the individual, however able, however earnest, strives in vain. Only the seeds of great dynamic ideas, sown over society and growing from the souls of men, can successfully cope with the frightful outcroppage of materialistic tares.

Now what are these ideas, capable of salting the democracy against the swarming germs of decay? In answer, it must first of all be pointed out that Whitman was not under the delusion that he could draw up the program for posterity. Posterity will itself know best along what lines to work out its social and moral salvation. But the knowledge of this fact does not prevent a serious and far-sighted spectator of democracy from making some provisional suggestions, which will indicate, in a general way, the quarter from which light may be expected.

It is in the great ideas that comprehend man's relation to nature and his fellows, the personality and its relation to the spiritual order of the universe, that Whitman finds the promise and potency of future spiritual and social renovation. The principal among these ideas are nature, comradeship, personality, the soul (or spiritual personality), the whole, faith, religion, death, immortality, right, God. Other ideas are easily deducible from these.

The nature, origin, and functions of most of these ideas—so far as they come within the scope of Whitman's work—have been already fully explained in the preceding pages. The idea of God will be treated in the next and last chapter. Religion will be considered in the following section. I must now say a few words on Whitman's developed idea of right.

It will be remembered that in examining Whitman's ethical ideas during the period of naturalism we found that he in effect subordinated the idea of right to the exigencies and intuitions of the personality; that his idea was naturalistic and rested largely on the biological point of view. That this tendency to substitute the biological for the ethical point of view was not merely a passing phase of his progressive evolution, but in a certain sense permanent, is evident from the remarks we have made in examining the influence of the idea of the whole on this tendency. We found that this idea of the whole, which had become perhaps the most important and shaping factor in his later thought, would of itself tend to the biological point of view. The conclusion is that the remarks which were made in Chapter 4 on the subject of Whitman's ethical ideas remain subsequently true for this period also. His biological standpoint, too, remained the same.

But it would be wrong to infer from this that there was no observable growth in this part of Whitman's thought. It would indeed be astonishing for a man to develop from the naturalistic to the spiritual point of view, and yet to have his ethical concepts unaffected by that development. Both naturalism and spiritualism are consistent with the biological as distinguished from the ethical point of view, though their practical results within the sphere of morality would often be very different.

In the period of naturalism his view of life and conduct was determined mainly by emotional conceptions. The passion and the practice of comradeship seemed to him a sufficient basis, not only for religion, but also for the right regulation of the individual and social life. But the evidence is clear that the spiritualistic advance of his personality was accompanied by a corresponding transcendence of the purely emotional point of view:

Great is emotional love, even in the order of the rational universe. But, if we must make gradations, I am clear that there is something greater. Power, love, veneration, products, genius, esthetics, tried by subtlest comparisons, analyses, and in serenest moods, somewhere fail, somehow become vain. Then noiseless, with flowing steps, the lord, the sun, the last ideal comes. By the names right, justice, truth, we suggest, but do not describe it. To the world of men it remains a dream, an idea, as they call it. But no dream is it to the wise—but the proudest, almost only solid lasting thing of all. Its analogy in the material universe is what holds together this world, and every object upon it, and carries its dynamics on forever sure and safe. Its lack, and the persistent shirking of it, as in life, sociology, literature, politics, business, and even sermonizing, these times, or any times, still leaves the abysm, the mortal flaw and smutch, mocking civilization today, with all its unquestion'd triumphs, and all the civilization so far known.[36]

In its purest and most exalted forms, this idea of right rises even above religion, in which there is, according to Whitman, a strong residuum of naturalism:

The climax of this loftiest range of civilization, rising above all the gorgeous shows and results of wealth, intellect, power, and art, as such—above even theology and religious fervor—is to be its development, from the eternal bases, and the fit expression, of absolute Conscience, moral soundness, Justice. Even in religious fervor there is a touch of animal heat. But moral conscientiousness, crystalline, without flaw, not Godlike only, entirely human, awes and enchants forever.[37]

He limits, however, the construction to be put on these dicta by saying that the absolute Conscience must move in harmony with "the general proportionate development of the whole man".

▶ *Great personalities shall arise whose work it shall be to make these ideas practical all-pervading forces in the future democracy.*

While it will be generally admitted that the spread of great ideas—such, for instance, as have already been mentioned—alone can effectively counteract the materialising tendencies of the industrial democratic regime, the question at once suggests itself how these ideas can be brought to the apprehension of the great mass of the people, who have no aptitude for ideas. The question is a formidable one, and must be faced by everyone who works for the spiritualisation of democracy. The coincidence is not a little remarkable that Carlyle and Whitman, with their absolutely divergent views of democracy, both arrived at conclusions on this point which have a certain general resemblance. Both finally fall back on the Great Man. Carlyle's ideas on the paramount question of heroes and their necessity for the ailing democracy are well known. It is generally felt that he went wrong when he insisted that the true hero must also be the strong man; must, in fact, become a politician, and exercise his influence from the high places of the earth. Not only had he the most quixotic views as to how the Great Man could be lifted to the top of the political hierarchy; he never seems to have asked himself the question, how many of the great epoch-making personalities of the world actually did attain to political pre-eminence. One cannot help feeling that, on this subject, the man who obtained his knowledge of the world almost solely from books was far more likely to go astray than the man who, with little Latin and less Greek, devoted his whole life to a study of the practical working of social and moral democracy.

Whitman's idea of the work of the great man is not that he should, by his superior intelligence and will, curb and morally (if not politically) enslave the common people for their so-called good. In his view the instruments of their efforts must be not coercive legislation and grandmotherly administration, but those great ideas that spring from the moral and spiritual personality. Like Christ, Whitman saw clearly that the spiritual personality alone is the immutable rockbed on which to plant the lever that is to raise human life to a higher level.

It will be the work of the great personalities that shall dominate the future democracy to realise and personalise, so far as possible, the highest ideas in themselves and thus bring them to the apprehension of the common people. By this personal realisation and incorporation of the great ideas that form the life-blood of the democracy, the great personalities will join the practical to the ideal; and thus become the personal links between the real and the ideal. They will be the great ideal-spiritual mediators of humanity. In regard to the function of those great personalities as incorporators of the invisible ideal, the following passage may be quoted:

Whatever may have been the case in years gone by, the true use for the imaginative faculty of modern times is to give ultimate vivification to facts, to science, and to common lives, endowing them with the glows and glories and final illustriousness which belong to every real thing, and to real things only. Without that ultimate vivification—which the poet or artist alone can give—reality itself would seem incomplete, and science, democracy, and life itself, finally in vain.[38]

It is only the great "cosmical artist-minds that can gauge the infinite meaning of the common people"; and their work it will be to condense and formulate the vague, nebulous thoughts, hopes, and aspirations of the common people. It will be for them to render practical and living the great ideas by identifying them in great imaginative creations; to endow literature with "great archetypal models of personalism" which shall feed and purify the flame of personality in the common people. Whitman calls these great imaginative achievements or forms in which the ideal will be incorporated "eidolons", and says:

The prophet and the bard,
Shall yet maintain themselves, in higher stages yet,
Shall mediate to the Modern, to Democracy, interpret yet to them
God and eidolons.[39]

It will be their prerogative to be free from the conventional standards of average society:

In fact [they] know no laws, but the laws of themselves, planted in them by God, and are themselves the last standards of the law, and its final exponents—responsible to Him directly, and not at all to mere etiquette. Often the best service that can be done to the race, is to lift the veil, at least for a time, from these rules and fossil-etiquettes.[40]

Both for its own independent interest and as a collateral indication of Whitman's personal evolution, it is worth while to look at the unfolding of the idea of the "great personality" in his work. The primary source of the idea is of course his own personality, of which it was merely the reflex.

The idea first appears in the great Preface to the first edition of *Leaves of Grass*. Indeed, that whole Preface may be described as the delineation of the great poet and his work in the future democracy. There the idea of the great poet is pervaded by the stormy and triumphant naturalism characteristic of that period. Only two passages can here be quoted; the first describing the great poet as the one complete lover and believer, the other describing him as the acme of sympathy and pride:

The known universe has one complete lover, and that is the greatest poet. He consumes an eternal passion, and is indifferent which chance happens, and which possible contingency of fortune or misfortune, and persuades daily and hourly his delicious pay . . . . His love above all love has leisure and expanse—he leaves room ahead of himself. He is no irresolute or suspicious lover— he is sure—he scorns intervals. His experience and the showers and thrills are not for nothing. Nothing can jar him—suffering and darkness cannot—death and fear cannot. To him complaint and jealousy and envy are corpses buried and rotten in the earth—he saw them buried. The sea is not surer of the shore, or the shore of the sea, than he is the fruition of his love, and of all perfection and beauty.[41]

The greatest poet does not only dazzle his rays over character and scenes and passions—he finally ascends, and finishes all—he exhibits the pinnacles that no man can tell what they are for, or what is beyond—he glows a moment on the extremest verge. He is most wonderful in his half-hidden smile or frown; by that flash of the moment of parting the one that sees it shall be encouraged or terrified afterward for many years. The greatest poet does not moralize or make applications of morals—he knows the soul. The soul has that measureless pride which consists in never acknowledging any lessons or deductions but its own. But it has sympathy as measureless as its pride, and the one balances the other, and neither can stretch too far while it stretches in company with the other. The inmost secrets of art sleep with the twain. The greatest poet has lain close betwixt both, and they are vital in his style and thoughts.[42]

These ideas of this Preface were afterwards incorporated into "By Blue Ontario's Shore".

We next meet the idea in the little poem "To Him That Was Crucified", appearing first in the edition of 1860, in which, putting himself for a moment on a level with Christ and other spiritual leaders of humanity, he says:

That we all labor together, transmitting the same charge and succession,
We few equals indifferent of lands, indifferent of times,
We, enclosers of all continents, all castes, allowers of all theologies,
Compassionaters, perceivers, rapport of men,
We walk silent, among disputes and assertions, but reject not the disputes nor anything that is asserted,
We hear the bawling and din, we are reach'd at by divisions, jealousies, recriminations on every side,
They close peremptorily upon us to surround us, my comrade,
Yet we walk unheld, free, the whole earth over, journeying up and down till we make our ineffaceable mark upon time and the diverse eras,
Till we saturate time and eras, that the men and women of races, ages to come, may prove brethren and lovers as we are.[43]

There is here a perceptible advance in spirituality on the Preface of 1855.

Then we have the idea of the great personality appearing in the band of cosmic teachers, divine literati, in "Democratic Vistas" in 1871. There the great personality is no longer a mere emotional link between the peoples and the ages, but the "inspired achiever", who shall interpret the spiritual world to democracy and "limn with absolute faith the mighty living Present".

Yet I have dream'd, merged in that hidden-tangled problem of our fate, whose long unravelling stretches mysteriously through time—dream'd out, portray'd, hinted already, a little or a larger band—a band of brave and true, unprecedented yet—arm'd and equipt at every point—the members separated, it may be, by different dates and States, or south, or north, or east, or west—Pacific, Atlantic, Southern, Canadian—a year, a century here, and other centuries there—but always one, compact in soul, conscience-conserving, God-inculcating, inspired achievers, not only in literature, the greatest art, but achievers in all art—a new undying order, dynasty, from age to age, transmitted—a band, a class, at least as fit to cope with current years, our dangers, needs, as those who, for their times, so long, so well, in armor or in cowl, upheld and made illustrious, that far-back feudal, priestly world.[44]

A little after that the idea of the great personality appears in "Passage to India" under the form of the "son of God". There he is no longer merely the great lover, and spiritual leader of democracy, but his spirit, insight, and passion embraces the whole universe. He shall "read the secret of impassive earth" and effect the last great reconciliation, after which the human mind is yearning, by absolutely fusing God and Nature. Thus the idea of the whole completes the rounding arch in the idea of the great personality.

Finally shall come the poet worthy the name,
The true son of God shall come singing his songs.

Then not your deeds only O voyagers, O scientists and inventors,
    shall be justified,
All these hearts as of fretted children shall be sooth'd,
All affection shall be fully responded to, the secret shall be told,
All these separations and gaps shall be taken up and hook'd and
    link'd together,
The whole earth, this cold, impassive, voiceless earth, shall be
    completely justified,
Trinitas divine shall be gloriously accomplish'd and compacted by
    the true son of God, the poet,
(He shall indeed pass the straits and conquer the mountains,
He shall double the cape of Good Hope to some purpose,)
Nature and Man shall be disjoin'd and diffus'd no more,
The true son of God shall absolutely fuse them.[45]

And finally, and starting from this absolute fusion and reconciliation of God, Man, and Nature, the great poet shall build up a new, vaster idea of God, the last and greatest idea of the human mind. But this falls within the last chapter.

Mystic Spiritualism

This section does not properly fall within the chapter on Applied Spiritualism; that is, spiritualism applied to such objective facts as democracy, personality, literature, etc. In character it resembles the matter that will be presented in the following chapter, but in date it belongs distinctly to this period. Perhaps it is most correct and suggestive to look upon this mystic spiritualism as a transition between the stages of applied and of pure spiritualism.

Let us pause for a moment at this point to look at the general drift of what has been said so far. We have seen the personality of Whitman developing through the various stages of naturalism and emotionalism, and entering the stage of spiritualism. We have seen how, starting from and founding on the real, the actual, the material, his thought rose ever higher till it finally culminates in the idea of the whole. But all that ideal and spiritual superstructure is still based on the real. The spiritual and realistic tendencies, being in fact the same, as we saw in Chapter 2, developed together in his mind; and the spiritual thus becomes, as it were, the flowering of the real in his mind. His highest conceptions of God, Man, and the spiritual universe are finally founded on facts, and tested by rigorous reference to such facts. In short, his spiritualism does not repudiate science, but is in strict harmony with, and complementary of, science or exact knowledge.

While this statement is very largely correct, it cannot have escaped the acute reader of the preceding pages that there is a slight—at first very slight, but gradually increasing—tendency in Whitman towards mysticism. The tendency never overcomes the other tendency for realism and sanity, but keeps hovering on its flanks with ever-increasing audacity. This spiritual-religious mysticism found at last expression in "Passage to India", published in 1871, the most important poem written during the early period of spiritualism. In point of poetic beauty, and as an indication of the direction of Whitman's development, it bears to this period the same relation that "Song of Myself" bears to the period of naturalism, and "When Lilacs Last in the Dooryard Bloom'd" bears to the period of emotionalism.

Perhaps mysticism is a natural phase in the evolution of the spiritual personality. But how shall I explain what I mean by mysticism? For it is one of those experiences of the mind which are more easily felt than expressed; which, besides, cannot be adequately expressed in terms of our other experiences. To some, mysticism means merely hazy thinking, and therefore a factor that ought to be eliminated from our rationalised experience. To such I cannot even attempt to explain the term. Then there are others, whose intellectual fibre has been so relaxed by unflagging emotional and religious stimulation that the attempt would be just as vain to make them understand that, after all, even mysticism must be a phase and development of the real—and no mere chasing of illusions of the astral plane.

Mysticism seems to be that stage in the evolution of a sanely developing personality in which the mind feels it necessary to put by its intellectual accoutrements and to ascend, on the wings of emotion and aspiration, to a higher region of experience. There comes a period in the life of the cosmic personality —that is, the personality which has realised the idea of the whole—when it tries to span Nature, God, and Man, not by the intellect, but by the dissolving spiritual aspirations; and the soul tries to feed on the deeper spiritual realities which it imagines to exist beyond and above phenomenal existence. The sublime allegory in the *Phaedrus,* in which Plato describes how the hungry soul rises in the cycles of existence until it reaches the apex from which it feeds on the cosmic panorama, gives perhaps as close a figurative indication of mysticism as is possible at the present stage of human development. And the following passage, quoted from Whitman's criticism of Emerson's works, shows that he had passed into the region of development in which mysticism naturally flourishes: "But in old or nervous or solemnest or dying hours, when one needs the impalpably soothing and vitalizing influences of abysmic Nature, or its affinities in literature or human society, and the soul resents the keenest mere intellection, they will not be sought for." [46]

Mysticism is thus distinguished from spiritualism by its greater remoteness from the elements of objective fact or of intellect. While spiritualism is the contemplation of the great ideas in the suffused glow of the emotional nature, mysticism is more the abandonment of the mind to the mysteries that surround and lie beyond those ideas. I have already pointed out that the significance of such states of mind is two-fold: they supply the natural environment for the spiritual personality and, besides, have a prophetic aspect. They show the vague and vast regions which, though not yet within the narrower circle of the intellect or reason, are already within the range of the consciousness and will probably become more distinct and formulable as the evolution of our race continues.

"Passage to India" was written on the occasion of the opening of the Suez Canal, which finally solved the old nautical problem of a shorter route to India. Its gist may be summarily stated as follows:

(1) This shorter passage to India is a mechanical triumph of man over a difficulty that had baffled his ingenuity and reckless daring for centuries.

(2) It is also a spiritual victory in that it brings Europe nearer to the East, the land of man's spiritual dawn.

(3) It is a symbol of the eternal voyage of the soul in its unbaffled aspiration towards the infinite.

As Europe and America are so far identified with the material and social progress of humanity, so Asia, with the shadows that brood over its mysterious past, is the birthplace and nursery of the soul. The poet, having devoted his life to glorifying the achievements of the modern world, now turns aside for a moment to pay his tribute to the oriental past:

The Past—the dark unfathom'd retrospect!
The teeming gulf—the sleepers and the shadows!

The past—the infinite greatness of the past!
For what is the present after all but a growth out of the past?
. . . .
Not you alone, proud truths of the world,
Nor you alone, ye facts of modern science,
But myths and fables of eld, Asia's, Africa's fables,
The far-darting beams of the spirit, the unloos'd dreams,
The deep-diving bibles and legends,
The daring plots of the poets, the elder religions;
O you temples fairer than lilies pour'd over by the rising sun!
O you fables spurning the known, eluding the hold of the known,
    mounting to heaven!
You lofty and dazzling towers, pinnacled, red as roses, burnish'd
    with gold!
Towers of fables immortal fashion'd from mortal dreams!
You too I welcome and fully the same as the rest!
You too with joy I sing.[47]

As the poet ponders over the endless failures of humanity
and its final success in discovering this shorter route, he says:
Surely, not only our mechanical efforts, but the vast, cosmic,
spiritual dreams of our race must also have "their hidden prophetic intention", finally somehow to be fulfilled!

O vast Rondure, swimming in space,
Cover'd all over with visible power and beauty,
Alternate light and day and the teeming spiritual darkness,
Unspeakable high processions of sun and moon and countless
    stars above,
Below, the manifold grass and waters, animals, mountains, trees,
With inscrutable purpose, some hidden prophetic intention,
Now first it seems my thought begins to span thee.[48]

The great questions of our destiny and the mysteries of our
march have an inexhaustible fascination for progressive humanity:

Ah who shall soothe these feverish children?
Who justify these restless explorations?
Who speak the secret of impassive earth?
Who bind it to us? what is this separate Nature so unnatural?

174

What is this earth to our affections? (unloving earth, without a
    throb to answer ours,
Cold earth, the place of graves.) [49]

The poet suggests that after science has faithfully accomplished its work

Finally shall come the poet worthy the name,
The true son of God shall come singing his songs.

He shall consummate the divine *trinitas* by reconciling man
with God, and God with nature.

As the poet contemplates this far-off destiny of our race, the
image of the past once more rises before him with

The flowing literatures, tremendous epics, religions, castes,
Old occult Brahma interminably far back, the tender and junior
    Buddha.

Then rises before him the vision of young Europe in 1492:

Something swelling in humanity now like the sap of the earth in
    spring,
The sunset splendor of chivalry declining.

He sees the sad shade of Columbus, and the other great navigators; he sees how the seed which they sowed, after centuries

Uprising in the night, it sprouts, blooms,
And fills the earth with use and beauty.

Now he sees that the voyage is far more than a merely earthly
one:

Passage indeed O soul to pimal thought,
Not lands and seas alone, thy own clear freshness,
The young maturity of brood and bloom,
To realms of budding bibles.

He calls upon his soul to set sail—"fearless for unknown
shores on waves of ecstasy to sail":

O soul, repressless, I with thee and thou with me,
Thy circumnavigation of the world begin,
Of man, the voyage of his mind's return,

To reason's early paradise,
Back, back to wisdom's birth, to innocent intuitions,
Again with fair creation.

. . . .

Bear me indeed as through the regions infinite,
Whose air I breathe, whose ripples hear, lave me all over,
Bathe me O God in thee, mounting to thee,
I and my soul to range in range of thee.

He thanks God that He has set no limits to the progress of
the soul; that the soul can compass the harmonious systems that
circle "Athwart the shapeless vastnesses of space"; that he can
ask the triumphant question:

What aspirations, wishes, outvie thine and ours O soul?
What dreams of the ideal? What plans of purity, perfection,
    strength?
What cheerful willingness for others' sake to give up all?
For others' sake to suffer all?

He seeks the rocks ahead on that far voyage:

Passage to you, your shores, ye aged fierce enigmas!
Passage to you, to mastership of you, ye strangling problems!
You, strew'd with the wrecks of skeletons, that, living, never reach'd
    you!

But he sees also the far haven beyond:

Reckoning ahead O soul, when thou, the time achiev'd,
The seas all cross'd, weather'd the capes, the voyage done,
Surrounded, copest, frontest God, yieldest, the aim attain'd,
As fill'd with friendship, love complete, the Elder Brother found,
The Younger melts in fondness in his arms.

At this point he gives orders that the anchors be instantly
hoisted, the hawsers cut, and every sail be shaken out:

Sail forth—steer for the deep waters only,
Reckless O soul, exploring, I with thee, and thou with me,
For we are bound where mariner has not yet dared to go,
And we will risk the ship, ourselves and all,

knowing that all the seas are God's.

Besides "Passage to India", there is a beautiful little poem called "A Riddle Song" which belongs to this or the following period, in which Whitman tries to express (I think) that un-nameable life pervading the cosmos, whose manifestations are variously called beauty, truth, or love; whose attraction for humanity is the cause of all the aspirations, and deathless efforts, and self-sacrifice of the race. It is instructive, and as it seems to be but little known, it may here be quoted in full:

That which eludes this verse and any verse,
Unheard by sharpest ear, unform'd in clearest eye or cunningest
    mind,
Nor lore nor fame, nor happiness nor wealth,
And yet the pulse of every heart and life throughout the world in-
    cessantly,
Which you and I and all pursuing ever ever miss,
Open but still a secret, the real of the real, an illusion,
Costless, vouchsafed to each, yet never man the owner,
Which poets vainly seek to put in rhyme, historians in prose,
Which sculptor never chisel'd yet, nor painter painted,
Which vocalist never sung, nor orator nor actor ever utter'd,
Invoking here and now I challenge for my song.

Indifferently, 'mid public, private haunts, in solitude,
Behind the mountain and the wood,
Companion of the city's busiest streets, through the assemblage,
It and its radiations constantly glide.

In looks of fair unconscious babes,
Or strangely in the coffin'd dead,
Or show of breaking dawn or stars by night,
As some dissolving delicate film of dreams,
Hiding yet lingering.

Two little breaths of words comprising it,
Two words, yet all from first to last comprised in it.

How ardently for it!
How many ships have sail'd and sunk for it!
How many travellers started from their homes and ne'er returned!

177

How much of genius boldly staked and lost for it!
What countless stores of beauty, love, ventur'd for it!
How all superbest deeds since Time began are traceable to it—and
    shall be to the end!
How all heroic martyrdoms to it!
How, justified by it, the horrors, evils, battles of the earth!
How the bright fascinating lambent flames of it, in every age and
    land, have drawn men's eyes,
Rich as a sunset on the Norway coast, the sky, the islands, and the
    cliffs,
Or midnight's silent glowing northern lights unreachable.

Haply God's riddle it, so vague and yet so certain,
The soul for it, and all the visible universe for it,
And heaven at last for it.

7

Period of Pure or Religious Spiritualism
(1873-1892)

Factors of Experience

"Halcyon Days"

Not from successful love alone,
Nor wealth, nor honor'd middle age, nor victories of politics or
    war;
But as life wanes, and all the turbulent passions calm,
As gorgeous, vapory, silent hues cover the evening sky,
As softness, fulness, rest, suffuse the frame, like fresher, balmier
    air,
As the days take on a mellower light, and the apple at last hangs
    really finish'd and indolent-ripe on the tree,
Then for the teeming quietest, happiest days of all!
The brooding and blissful halcyon days!

We have now arrived at the last stage of the evolution of
Whitman's personality—perhaps the most interesting of all, as
it certainly is the most difficult to describe. We saw how the
eternal life-process, converging to a centre, gave birth to his
fluid personality. We saw how that personality, having differentiated itself from its source, began to develop along its own
independent lines, according to its own germinal form. Then
we saw it traverse the successive cycles or stages of the natural
personality, the emotional personality, and the cosmic person-

ality. In the cosmic stage his personality once more approaches the cosmic process—that ocean of real or potential life from which it was originally differentiated and disengaged. In this last stage we shall see the maturity of his spiritual personality; the personality here enters that world of "resistless spiritual gravitation" where the assimilation of object and subject enters upon its last apparent phase; and the harmonisation of the human individual, the part, with the whole is carried beyond the plane of material existence. In the last section of the preceding chapter we saw Whitman's personality enter the regions of the higher spiritual sphere as a mystic, an unknown territory, where thought and feeling both give place to the ecstatic vision in which the young soul surveys its goodly heritage. In this chapter we shall see how the shadows of that mystic world gradually clear away and become transparent; how the soul, after the first raptures of its new experience, begins to realise its new position and surroundings; becomes aware of the greater and larger ideas circling in the azure of that serener atmosphere, and begins to feel that they are no phantasmagory, but only a higher reality.

The factors of experience at this stage of his development are easily told. The collapse of his system which, as we saw, had begun in 1864 already, finally culminated in a severe paralytic attack in 1873. He had to give up his work as a clerk in the civil service at Washington and to retire to Camden, New Jersey, where the next three years of his life were spent. The loss of his mother through death at the end of 1873 was such a shock to his already shattered system that it finally rendered vain all hope of his recovery. How passionately he was attached to her is attested by numerous beautiful touches and references in his works. Through good report and evil she had kept her faith, not only in his personal greatness, but also in the significance of his work. And the intensity of the passion he felt for her measured the magnitude of the loss he sustained by her death. The lines in which he commemorates her death may be quoted here:

As at thy portals also death,
Entering thy sovereign, dim, illimitable grounds,
To memories of my mother, to the divine blending, maternity,

To her, buried and gone, yet buried not, gone not from me,
(I see again the calm benignant face fresh and beautiful still,
I sit by the form in the coffin;
I kiss and kiss convulsively again the sweet old lips, the cheeks,
    the closed eyes in the coffin;)
To her, the ideal woman, practical, spiritual, of all of earth, life,
    love, to me the best,
I grave a monumental line, before I go, amid these songs,
And set a tombstone here.[1]

Several of the little poems of this period are directly inspired by his physical condition. Take, for instance, that one in which he evidently compares himself—the physical giant of bygone days—to a dismantled ship:

In some unused lagoon, some nameless bay,
On sluggish, lonesome waters, anchor'd near the shore,
An old, dismasted, gray and batter'd ship, disabled, done,
After free voyages to all the seas of earth, haul'd up at last and
    hawser'd tight,
Lies rusting, mouldering.[2]

But the pathos of the change appears most strikingly in the "Prayer of Columbus", which has also an obvious personal reference.

It was only in 1876 that he began slowly to recover from helpless prostration. As soon as he was able to move about some distance, he used to go "to a charmingly recluse and rural spot along Timber creek, twelve or thirteen miles from where it enters the Delaware river".[3] He says in *Specimen Days* that half his time was thus spent in the country, and that it was this contact with vital outdoor nature that helped his system to a partial recovery. From this time the jottings in *Specimen Days* are resumed, so that we are able to gauge thereby the influence of his experience on his further development.

The brilliant sun of naturalism had set; the deeper afternoon tints of emotionalism had gradually faded into the hushed twilight of declining life. As the lengthening shadows of depressed vitality gave way to the gathering darkness and final gloom of physical prostration, the ideas, the spiritual intuitions of the personality, rose ever clearer and brighter in the cosmic heaven. The whirlwind of passion had blown past; the deadly frost of pain and doubt had done its worst. But beyond storm and frost, beyond the far, mystic depths of night, those spiritual stars were shining, radiating their voiceless inspiration to the soul; and around, the brooding hush of nature, scarce broken by the silver tone of bird or streamlet's wandering sibilation, sank with the balm of peace divine into the soul. And through the night the child's sobbing of the lonely soul was heard responsive: "To God and Nature". These now become the great subjects of Whitman's thought and experience. "Away from society, and back to primeval Nature, and through Nature back to God" now becomes the keynote of his work. "Away then", he says,

to loosen, to unstring the divine bow, so tense, so long. Away, from curtain, carpet, sofa, book—from "society"—from city house, street, and modern improvements and luxuries—away to the primitive winding, aforementioned wooded creek, with its untrimm'd bushes and turfy banks—away from ligatures, tight boots, buttons, and the whole cast-iron civilizee life—from entourage of artificial store, machine, studio, office, parlor—from tailordom and fashion's clothes —from any clothes, perhaps, for the nonce, the summer heats advancing, there in those watery, shaded solitudes. Away, thou soul, (let me pick thee out singly, reader dear, and talk in perfect freedom, negligently, confidentially,) for one day and night at least, returning to the naked source-life of us all—to the breast of the great silent savage, all-acceptive Mother. Alas! how many of us are so sodden, how many have wander'd so far away, that return is almost impossible.[4]

In another passage he explains:

> Away from Books—away from Art,
> Now for the Day and Night—the lesson done,
> Now for the Sun and Stars.[5]

How lovingly, and with what profound interest, he now began to study the phenomena of physical nature appears from *Specimen Days;* the birds and trees, the brooks and bees are all commemorated there with amusing picturesqueness and detail.

But above all, the night fascinated him. The descriptions of night which occur in *Specimen Days* are probably among the most brilliant and beautiful ever written. To him the night was filled with infinite suggestion. Thus, after a very striking picture of a summer night in 1878 (too long to be quoted here) he describes its effect on him in the following passage:

As if for the first time, indeed, creation noiselessly sank into and through me its placid and untellable lesson, beyond—O, so infinitely beyond!—anything from art, books, sermons, or from science, old or new. The spirit's hour—religion's hour—the visible suggestion of God in space and time—now once definitely indicated, if never again. The untold pointed at—the heavens all paved with it. The Milky Way, as if some superhuman symphony, some ode of universal vagueness, disdaining syllable and sound—a flashing glance of Deity, address'd to the soul. All silently—the indescribable night and stars—far off and silently.[6]

The renovative influence of the sky on him is shown by another passage, rendered pathetic by the unusual tone of the allusion to his own condition: "Hast Thou, pellucid, in Thy azure depths, medicine for case like mine? (Ah, the physical shatter and troubled spirit of me the last three years.) And dost Thou subtly mystically now drip it through the air invisibly upon me?"[7]

Yet sometimes the old note of passion is heard again in these descriptions of night:

Overhead, the splendor indescribable; yet something haughty, almost supercilious, in the night. Never did I realize more latent sentiment, almost *passion,* in those silent interminable stars up there. One can understand, such a night, why, from the days of the Pharaohs or Job, the dome of heaven, sprinkled with planets, has supplied the subtlest, deepest criticism on human pride, glory, ambition.[8]

Religion

This return from the distracting life of society, from the passions and emotions that strain the personality on the social plane, to the primal simplicity and sanity of mother nature, was at the same time an entrance into the higher and highest sphere of the spiritual world; was the means whereby the spiritual personality developed towards its final earthly consummation. This is undoubtedly a mere statement of fact in Whitman's case. But as there is probably a general significance in it, I venture to make a few remarks preliminary and introductory to the proper inquiry of this chapter.

Through all ages, but especially in our own, the tragic isolation of the personality has been a favourite theme with the finer spirits among writers. Who does not know the impenetrable prison walls of the personality against which the wings of the soul beat in vain! Who has not felt the agony of loneliness which the mind sometimes endures, in moments of trouble and joy alike, because no craving for sympathy (however intense), no desire to sympathise (however deeply felt), can carry the isolated soul beyond and outside of itself!

Schiller expresses this experience epigrammatically in two lines which I quote from memory:

Warum kann der lebendige Geist nicht dem Geiste erscheinen?
Spricht die Seele, so spricht, ach! Schon die Seele nicht mehr.[9]

Are there not times in the life of every one when the soul longs with an irrepressible longing to pour itself forth in love, or aspiration, or adoration; to pass, if but for a single moment, beyond its own adamantine limits and to merge itself in the object or objects of its passion? And if every one has such times, they are probably the bitterest and most agonising in the experience of those lofty spirits who habitually live in an atmosphere beyond that of common humanity.

But, looked at from another point of view, this most painful experience is the source of all that is most exalted and pure in the life of the soul. These bitter pangs are the true birth of the spiritual personality. It is only when the personality has lived its social life and has thus gauged the painful imperfection and limitation of its means of communication with the world around it; it is only when it begins to realise that its deepest experiences cut it off from the world of society, of love and comradeship and sympathy; it is then only that the personality begins to long for the ideal or divine comradeship in life. In moments of deepest love and aspiration, of bitterest remorse and repentance, when the personality ascends the unfrequented pinnacles of its being, the divine germ begins to develop in the personality; the ideal becomes the most real and satisfying. In other words, the individual personality is the purest and perhaps only source of our highest religious intuitions and experiences. This truth has been expressed by Whitman in a passage which ought to become the *locus classicus* on the subject:

The ripeness of Religion is doubtless to be looked for in this field of individuality, and is a result that no organization or church can ever achieve. . . . Religion, although casually arrested and, after a fashion, preserv'd in the churches and creeds, does not depend at all upon them, but is a part of the identified soul, which, when greatest, knows not bibles in the old way, but in new ways— the identified soul, which can really confront Religion when it extricates itself entirely from the churches, and not before. Personalism fuses this, and favors it. I should say, indeed, that only in the perfect uncontamination and solitariness of the individuality may the spirituality of religion positively come forth at all. Only here, and on such terms, the meditation, the devout ecstasy, the soaring flight. Only here, communion with the mysteries, the eternal problems, whence? whither? Alone, and identity, and the mood—and the soul emerges, and all statements, churches, sermons, melt away like vapors. Alone, and silent thought and awe, and aspiration—and then the interior consciousness, like a hitherto unseen inscription, in magic ink, beams out its wondrous lines to the sense. Bibles may convey, and priests expound; but it is exclusively for the noiseless operation of one's isolated Self, to enter the pure ether of veneration, reach the divine levels, and commune with the unutterable.[10]

Looking now from this height of religion, one can measure the vast progress made by Whitman's personality since the first publication of *Leaves of Grass*. In "Song of Myself" we saw the individual current in full force; we saw the self-satisfaction and self-elation of the individual personality, little dreaming that there was yet an unthought progress before it. In 1860 another tendency—the social element—becomes conspicuous; the individual personality of "Song of Myself" yields to the social gravitation of "Calamus". This tendency towards the socialisation of the personality reaches its extreme limit in the period of emotionalism, where it sometimes seems as if the bands of the personality are beginning to snap. But in the period of calm and thoughtfulness that followed, the individual personality began to rise by the very steps of experience, which the social personality had laid down, to a greater height and dominance over its antagonist. And it is in this final stage in the evolution of the individual personality that the religious intuitions attain their last and purest forms. In the last chapter we saw the germ of this loftier spiritualism still traversing the strata of society, democracy, and literature. In this chapter it rises beyond them and enters its last and highest environment— the pure ideal world.

A curious, but by no means peculiar, indication of the renewed interest which Whitman began to feel, in the evening of his life, in religious subjects, is afforded us by several sections in "November Boughs". The study of Elias Hicks, the Quaker, in particular shows that the subject which had interested his early childhood was again engaging his attention in old age. How far the Quaker theory of the "Inner Light", which he had heard expounded in early boyhood by the eloquent Hicks, had helped to shape his own opinions, it is difficult to say. But in old age he substantially endorses this view as in harmony with his own, and with the universal needs of the highest spiritual life. He concludes an account of a lecture by Hicks with these remarks:

Now and then . . . he was very mystical and radical, and had much to say of "the light within." Very likely this same *inner light,* (so dwelt upon by newer men as by Fox and Barclay at the beginning, and all Friends and deep thinkers since and now,) is perhaps only another name for the religious conscience. In my opinion they have all diagnos'd, like superior doctors, the real inmost disease of our times, probably any times. Amid the huge inflammation call'd society, and that other inflammation call'd politics, what is there to-day of moral power and ethic sanity as antiseptic to them and all? . . . Elias taught throughout, as George Fox began it, or rather reiterated and verified it, the Platonic doctrine that the ideals of character, of justice, of religious action, whenever the highest is at stake, are to be conform'd to no outside doctrine of creeds, Bibles, legislative enactments, conventionalities, or even decorums, but are to follow the inward Deity-planted law of the emotional Soul. In this only the true Quaker, or Friend, has faith.[11]

The Cosmic Theology

From this religious point of view Whitman indicates generally the work which must still be done in the departments of science, metaphysics, and theology. Among others he criticises the Darwinian theory. Great as are the services of Darwinism to scientific thought, he anticipates the day when evolution will no longer dominate everything else, but assume its true place as but a segment in the full circle of biological knowledge. In the theory—handed down by the religious traditions of many peoples from the hoariest antiquity—of the divine descent of man, there is a profound truth, and it will be the work of the great biological metaphysicians of the future to reconcile Darwinism with this primeval tradition; to show how man, starting from lowliest and humblest origin, rises gradually towards the divine pinnacles of his destiny. It is only when the great facts and theories of exact science become the basis for this spiritual superstructure; when science—instead of making havoc among the great religious ideas of the race—supports them and opens the vistas to still greater ideas, that it will perform its truest and greatest function in the disciplining culture of humanity.

Science, thus advancing from the facts of physical and biological nature to the facts of our spiritual consciousness, to the experiences, hopes, fears, aspirations, and ideas of the human soul, will finally culminate in the new spiritual theology. Real as are our physical experiences, the phenomena of our spiritual life are far more real still in that they touch deeper chords in our manifold nature. And to the great workers of the future is assigned the task of interpreting these phenomena in harmony with our physical experiences, and thus crowning cosmic science with a cosmic theology, ampler and diviner far than any yet known. He writes, in 1876:

Only (for me, at any rate, in all my prose and poetry,) joyfully accepting modern science, and loyally following it without the slightest hesitation, there remains ever recognized still a higher flight, a higher fact, the eternal soul of man, (of all else too,) the spiritual, the religious—which it is to be the greatest office of scientism, in my opinion, and of future poetry also, to free from fables, crudities and superstitions, and launch forth in renew'd faith and scope a hundred fold. To me, the worlds of religiousness, of the conception of the divine, and of the ideal, though mainly latent, are just as absolute in humanity and the universe as the world of chemistry, or anything in the objective worlds. . . .

To me, the crown of savantism is to be, that it surely opens the way for a more splendid theology, and for ampler and diviner songs. No year, nor even century, will settle this. There is a phase of the real, lurking behind the real, which it is all for. There is also in the intellect of man, in time, far in prospective recesses, a judgment, a last appellate court, which will settle it.[12]

The greatest idea in theology, and indeed in all human thought, is the idea of God. It follows, therefore, that the idea of God will become the greatest subject for future metaphysical and theological study.

The Idea of God

Before giving an account of the evolution of the divine idea in Whitman's mind and work, I beg to indicate what I consider to be the true metaphysical position of that idea. Though this may seem at first sight to be going rather beyond the scope of this book, it will be seen immediately that I am only developing what has been said in Chapters 1 and 6, and am in fact defining Whitman's own opinions. Perhaps the matter may be stated thus: *the Platonic idea, the Baconian form, the Hegelian* Idee, *and the idea of the whole in Whitman are ultimately identical, and are the true basis of the idea of God.*

That the first three conceptions are identical has already been indicated in a general way in Chapter 1, and can no doubt be proved more or less rigorously. Coming, then, to Whitman's idea of the whole as explained in Chapter 6, I need only repeat that it is this: the whole—of anything—conceived as pervaded by an immanent life or spirit; as bound together by the same unifying agency or central coordinative power; as the expression of the same inner evolutionary being or existence. I have shown what important consequences follow from this conception when applied to the cosmos and to society. Now, on comparing this conception with the Hegelian *Idee,* it becomes at once evident that both of them involve the same root-element; and the same may be said in reference to the Platonic idea and the Baconian form.

Let me here refer, in passing, to a matter of great importance. If these four ideas are ultimately the same, a conclusion of the greatest importance to the underlying theory of this book follows. I have *assumed* in Chapter 1 that the first three ideas indicate the very nature of the personality. But I have also proved in Chapter 6 that the idea of the whole is substantially the outgrowth and expression of Whitman's personality. If, then, the idea of the whole is identical with the other three, it follows that the above assumption has been proved in the case of Whitman. Algebraic symbols will render the argument still clearer. Suppose Plato's idea is represented by a, Bacon's form by b, Hegel's *Idee* by c, and Whitman's idea of the whole by d. Suppose, also, P represents personality in general; P_1 represents Whitman's personality: then $a = b = c = d$.

But in Chapter 6 the idea of the whole was the outcome and expression of α, Whitman's personality; or $d\alpha P_1$. Hence $a = b = c = d\alpha P$.

In other words, in the particular case of Whitman, the root-element in all the four conceptions indicates the very nature of the personality.

But further: these four identical conceptions form the very basis of the divine idea. This dictum is naturally intended to be merely an expression of my own personal opinion. But I submit, with the greatest deference and diffidence, that in this identification of the most significant idea in philosophy with the personality on the one hand, and the idea of God on the other, we not only establish the basis of a far more fruitful psychology than that at present in vogue, but we further lay the metaphysical cornerstone of the temple of future theology—a temple, not the particular property of any one people or set of peoples, but dedicated to the use of humanity; to which all the tribes of men may resort with equal freedom and propriety. When God is thus conceived as the immanent life or spirit of the universe and humanity and personality, considered as a whole; as at once the dynamic evolutionary force underlying the infinite forms of existence and being, and the perfect end towards which that process is directed, the gulf between the natural and the supernatural is bridged; the primary conception of religion is seen to be but the spiritual form of the most indestructible idea in the whole of Western philosophical speculation. From a philosophic point of view, we obtain in this way a result towards which the most earnest endeavours of thinkers during this century have been directed—namely, the harmonising in the divine idea of the apparently discordant elements of cosmical immanence and personality. From a practical point of view, we get an idea of God which is not only in harmony with the best results of biological and philosophical thought, but in consonance also with the dictates of human consciousness and spiritual needs, and with the teachings of the most elevated forms of practical religion. For if God is conceived as the life of the whole, including the material and biological universe, including moreover humanity and the human personality, that life must necessarily involve the element of personality, extended to and harmonised with the entire universe of existence. Thus, too, we obtain a clue to the solution of the problem of evil. For, as I have shown in Chapter 6, evil or wrong is of the part; the whole is spiritual or holy (as the etymology shows), is hale or sane, and lifted above ethical distinctions. I need not say more here, as Whitman's idea of God was ultimately substantially the same as that here indicated, and passages will be quoted to show what meaning he read into that idea.

Coming now to the evolution of the divine idea in his mind, I may point out that Whitman's reticence on this most profound of subjects, especially in the earlier periods of his development, makes it very difficult to give any satisfactory account of the matter. We have seen already that he laid down in the 1855 Preface to *Leaves of Grass* that the great poet "would not argue with God"; and the great poet was the ideal in whose footsteps he was assiduously following. In the absence of explicit statements we have consequently to rely on hints. That, in some vague way, he early identified the divine idea with the cosmos, is perhaps no very violent assumption, though there is no direct authority for the statement.

The first hints refer to God under the form of the Comrade, after whom the soul is aspiring or longing. Thus, in "Song of Myself", he says in a passage already quoted:

My rendezvous is appointed, it is certain,
The Lord will be there and wait till I come on perfect terms,
The great Camerado, the lover true for whom I pine will be there.

This conception of God as the perfect comrade runs through all his earlier work. God, in fact, is for him the perfect expression of the natural, social, and emotional personality. He strikes a deeper note as the years roll on and his personality deepens, but it relates always to the divine comrade.

In "Passage to India" (1871) we first hear the vaster note:

O Thou transcendent,
Nameless, the fibre, and the breath,
Light of the light, shedding forth universes, thou centre of them,
Thou mightier centre of the true, the good, the loving,
Thou moral, spiritual fountain—affection's source—thou reservoir,
(O pensive soul of me—O thirst unsatisfied—waitest not there?
Waitest not haply for us somewhere there the Comrade perfect?)
Thou pulse—thou motive of the stars, suns, systems,
That, circling, move in order, safe, harmonious,
Athwart the shapeless vastnesses of space.[13]

Here God is no longer merely the emotional and spiritual fountain of the personality, but also the centre, fibre, breath of the whole universe.

After this comes the "Song of the Universal", in which the idea of the whole first finds expression, clear and unequivocal, thus becoming the foundation of the cosmic faith.

In "Chanting the Square Deific" we see another application of this extension of the idea of God. There the ultimate forces of life are coordinated into a larger conception of the divine whole.

In "A Riddle Song" the various aspects of this vast immanent cosmic life are superbly handled.

Finally, we have the beautiful little poem called "Gods", in which the divine idea includes not only the divine lover and comrade and the ideal man, but also the universal forms of experience and existence and the great ideas and aspirations of the race. I quote it in full:

> Lover divine and perfect Comrade,
> Waiting content, invisible yet, but certain,
> Be thou my God.
>
> Thou, thou, the Ideal Man,
> Fair, able, beautiful, content, and loving,
> Complete in body and dilate in spirit,
> Be thou my God.
>
> O Death, (for Life has served its turn,)
> Opener and usher to the heavenly mansion,
> Be thou my God.
>
> Aught, aught of mightiest, best I see, conceive, or know,
> (To break the stagnant tie—thee, thee to free, O soul,)
> Be thou my God.
>
> All great ideas, the races' aspirations,
> All heroisms, deeds of rapt enthusiasts,
> Be ye my Gods.

> Or Time and Space
> Or shape of Earth divine and wondrous,
> Or some fair shape I viewing, worship,
> Or lustrous orb of sun or star by night,
> Be ye my Gods.

This little poem—so profound in passion, so lofty in spirituality, so simple in structure, so vast in conception—is not only a striking instance of Whitman's unique poetic power, but gives probably the fullest statement of the idea of God considered as the spirit of the whole which it is possible to give. It may fitly crown his great achievements in thought and art. But it would not be in consonance with the spirit of Walt Whitman to conclude this account of his personal evolution with the quotation of an achieved result. The last word in Whitman is not attainment, but rather unattainment; and it is therefore in harmony with his own spirit to conclude this book by quoting a passage—one of the last he ever wrote—in which he indicates, not what has been done, but what still remains undone in this highest department of human thought and effort. After mentioning that Shakespeare and George Fox, the Quaker, sprang from the same social stratum and nearly at the same time, he concludes with the following pregnant remarks:

What is poor plain George Fox, compared to William Shakspere —to fancy's lord, imagination's heir? Yet George Fox stands for something too—a thought—the thought that wakes in silent hours —perhaps the deepest, most eternal thought latent in the human soul. This is the thought of God, merged in the thoughts of moral right and the immortality of identity. Great, great is this thought— aye, greater than all else. When the gorgeous pageant of Art, refulgent in the sunshine, color'd with roses and gold—with all the richest mere poetry, old and new, (even Shakspere's)—with all that statue, play, painting, music, architecture, oratory, can effect, ceases to satisfy and please—when the eager chase after wealth flags, and beauty itself becomes a loathing; and when all worldly or carnal or esthetic, or even scientific values, having done their office to the human character, and minister'd their part to its development—

then, if not before, comes forward this over-arching thought, and brings its eligibilities, germinations. Most neglected in life of all humanity's attributes, easily cover'd with crust, deluded and abused, rejected, yet the only certain source of what all are seeking, but few or none find—in it I for myself clearly see the first, the last, the deepest depths and highest heights of art, of literature, and of the purposes of life. I say whoever labors here, makes contributions here, or best of all sets an incarnated example here, of life or death, is dearest to humanity—remains after the rest are gone.[14]

Notes

*

(The notes provided by Smuts are indicated by the notation (S).)

Foreword

1. R. G. Menzies, *The Changing Commonwealth: The Smuts Memorial Lecture* (Cambridge: Cambridge University Press, 1960), p. 1.
2. W. K. Hancock, *Smuts: The Sanguine Years, 1870–1919* (Cambridge: Cambridge University Press, 1962), p. 48.
3. Ibid.
4. Jean van der Poel and W. K. Hancock, eds., *Selections from the Smuts Papers* (Cambridge: Cambridge University Press, 1962), 1: 52–53.
5. Ibid., 1: 53–54.
6. Ibid., 1: 54–56.
7. Ibid., 2: 13.
8. J. C. Smuts, *Jan Christian Smuts: A Biography* (New York: William Morrow, 1952), p. 19.
9. Ibid.
10. Hancock, pp. 49–50.

Chapter 1

1. A particular proof of its correctness will be given in Chapter 7. The general proof falls beyond the scope of this work. (S)
2. "Starting from Paumanok," 233–36.

Chapter 2

1. The whole subject is interestingly treated in Goethe's *Gott und Welt.* (S) The quotation, from *Urworte: Orphische,* is to be found in the section entitled "Dämon," and can be translated as

   > And no time and no power can shatter
   > Created form, which develops as it lives.

2. In a letter to Robert Southey (7 April 1819), Wordsworth wrote: "The Poem of Peter Bell, as the Prologue will show, was composed under a belief that the Imagination not only does not require for its exercise

the intervention of supernatural agency, but that, though such agency be excluded, the faculty may be called forth as imperiously, and for kindred results of pleasure, by incidents within the compass of poetic probability, in the humblest departments of life." The most succinct characterization of Peter Bell is to be found in the following lines:

> He roved among the vales and streams,
> In the green wood and hollow dell;
> They were his dwellings night and day,
> But nature ne'er could find the way
> Into the heart of Peter Bell.
>
> In vain, through every changeful year,
> Did Nature lead him as before;
> A primrose by a river's brim
> A yellow primrose was to him,
> And it was nothing more.
> "Peter Bell," 241–50.

3. See *Leaves of Grass*, "There Was a Child Went Forth." (S)

Chapter 3

1. John Burroughs, *Notes on Walt Whitman as Poet and Person* (New York: American News Company, 1867).
2. "In Cabin'd Ships at Sea," 10–17.
3. "With Husky-Haughty Lips, O Sea," 20–23.
4. "Sea Shore Fancies."
5. "Proud Music of the Storm," 59–70.

Chapter 4

1. "A Backward Glance O'er Travel'd Roads," 55–69.
2. "Song of Myself," 1148–68.
3. Ibid., 1202–09.
4. Ibid., 1198–1200.
5. Ibid., 1–3.
6. "One's-Self I Sing," 1–2.
7. "I Heard It Was Charged Against Me."
8. "Song of Myself," 43–44.
9. Ibid., 1309–13.
10. "By Blue Ontario's Shore," 288–90.
11. "As I Lay with My Head in Your Lap Camerado."
12. "Song of the Exposition," 1–3.
13. "By Blue Ontario's Shore," 43–46.
14. *Faust*, II, 11936–38 (*Goethes Werke* [Hamburg: Wegner, 1962], 1: 359). Dr. Hermann Reske, in his *Faust: Ein Einführung* (Berlin: Kohlham-

mer, 1971), emphasizes the need, in order to understand Goethe's viewpoint correctly, to include the following four lines:

Und hat an ihm die Liebe gar
Von oben teilgenommen,
Gegegnet ihm die selige Schar
Mit herzlichem Willkommen.

The six lines, spoken by angels floating in the higher atmosphere, carrying the immortal part of Faust, can be translated as:

Who never ceases struggling and striving
He we can redeem.
And if also love from above
Has participated,
Then the blessed throng will greet him
With heartfelt welcome.

15. "Song of the Open Road," 149–87.
16. "Faces," 46–47.
17. "Song of the Open Road," 220–24.
18. "Song of Myself," 506–15.
19. "From Noon to Starry Night," 54–59.
20. "Song of Myself," 463–67.
21. "Starting from Paumanok," 98–101.
22. See the footnote to "Democratic Vistas," 1686. (S)
23. "Song of Myself," 647–50.
24. *Specimen Days,* "Nature and Democracy—Morality," 18–22.
25. "Democratic Vistas," 1687–1700.
26. *Specimen Days,* "Edgar Poe's Significance," 53–56.
27. "Song of the Answerer," 71–72.
28. "Preface, 1872, to 'As a Strong Bird on Pinions Free'," 85–97.
29. "Starting from Paumanok," 69–70; 129–30; 105–13.
30. "Democratic Vistas," 1585–87.
31. This aphorism of Goethe (Introduction to *Faust,* I, 14) may be translated: "The course of human lives is as confused as a labyrinth."
32. Roaming in thought over the Universe, I saw the little that is
Good steadily hastening towards immortality,
And the vast all that is call'd Evil I saw hastening to merge itself
and become lost and dead.
"Roaming in Thought. (After reading HEGEL)." (S)
33. Smuts's marginal reference is "L.G. 362." This page contains the second half of "All is Truth" and the first half of "A Riddle Song."
34. "A Child's Amaze."
35. "To Think of Time," 101–07.
36. "Song of Myself," 1317–18.

37. These lines are from the poem, "To the Actor Krüger," dated 31 March 1827, sent with a presentation copy of *Iphigenia*, and may be translated as:

> All human frailties
> Are forgiven by pure humanity.

38. "I Sing the Body Electric," 124–28.
39. "A Memorandum at a Venture," 69–82.
40. Ibid., 55–64.
41. "Preface, 1876—*Leaves of Grass* and *Two Rivulets*," footnote to line 11, 159–67.
42. "A Song of Joys," 23.
43. "Of the Terrible Doubt of Appearances," 11–16.
44. "Recorders Ages Hence," 3–10.
45. "The Base of All Metaphysics."
46. "Democratic Vistas," footnote to line 1647.
47. "For You O Democracy," 1–9.
48. "Democratic Vistas," 528–607. (S)
49. "Thou Mother with Thy Equal Brood," 47–57.

Chapter 5

1. These lines, from *Wilhelm Meisters Lehrjahre* (1795), are sung by the wandering harper, who proves to be Mignon's father, and are overheard by Wilhelm. They may be translated as:

> Who never ate his bread with tears,
> Who never spent a night of sorrow
> Upon his bed in grief and fears,
> Knows you not, you heavenly power.

In his *Note to Goethe's Poems*, 1: 191, James Boyd writes: "The peculiar interest of these verses is that they express, with sublime beauty and masterly brevity, a theme which seems to have busied Goethe's mind and recurs in several works of the period; namely, the relentless, inexorable nature of fate."

2. W. D. O'Connor, *The Good Gray Poet: A Vindication* (New York: Bunce and Huntington, 1866), pp. 1–2, and reprinted in R. M. Bucke, *Walt Whitman* (Philadelphia: McKay, 1883), pp. 99–130.
3. "Preface, 1855—*Leaves of Grass*," 196–211.
4. *Specimen Days*, "My Preparations for Visits."
5. Ibid., "Back to Washington," 15–28.
6. Ibid., "Hospital Scenes and Persons," 1–3.
7. Ibid., "An Army Hospital Ward," 12–20.
8. Ibid., "A New York Soldier."
9. Ibid., "Soldiers and Talks," 1–11; 22–25.

10. *November Boughs,* "Last of the War Cases," 176–81.
11. *Specimen Days,* "Unnamed Remains the Bravest Soldier."
12. Ibid., "Three Years Summ'd Up."
13. Ibid., "Spiritual Characters among the Soldiers."
14. "I Dream'd in a Dream."
15. "Reconciliation."
16. "Ashes of Soldiers," 28–41.
17. *Specimen Days,* "Death of President Lincoln," 2–19.
18. See "The Weather—Does It Sympathize with These Times?" (S)
19. Of the coffin. (S)
20. This will be treated more fully in the next chapter. (S)
21. "Origins of Attempted Secession," 10–53.
22. Smuts provides as a footnote the whole poem, "Long, Too Long, America":

> Long, too long America,
> Traveling roads all even and peaceful you learn'd from joys and
>   prosperity only,
> But now, ah now, to learn from crises of anguish, advancing,
>   grappling with direst fate and recoiling not,
> And now to conceive and show to the world what your children
>   en-masse really are,
> (For who except myself has yet conceiv'd what your children
>   en-masse really are?)

23. *Specimen Days,* "National Uprising and Volunteering."
24. "Year That Trembled and Reel'd Beneath Me."
25. "Democratic Vistas," 1870–79.
26. *Specimen Days,* "The Real War Will Never Get in the Books," 1–11.

Chapter 6
1. "Song of Myself," 524–26.
2. There is no indication of it before 1865 in his works. (S)
3. "Starting from Paumanok," 170–74.
4. "Song of the Universal," 171–74.
5. Ibid., 8–9.
6. Ibid., 25–41.
7. *Specimen Days,* "Carlyle from American Points of View," 131–48.
8. "Preface, 1855, to first issue of *Leaves of Grass,*" 290–91. The line, "Sanity and ensemble characterize the great master," is the opening of the uncollected manuscript fragment now known by the short title "Sanity and Ensemble," and described by Blodgett and Bradley as "Probably not a poem, but an outline of ideas to be expanded into a poem that never got written, although the mood faintly suggests 'A Song of the Rolling Earth'." (Harold W. Blodgett and Sculley Bradley,

eds., *Leaves of Grass,* Comprehensive Reader's Edition [New York: New York University Press, 1965], p. 701 n.). The second passage is a paraphrase of the lines (219–24) in "Carlyle from American Points of View" which read:

> In short (to put it in our own form, summing up,) that thinker or analyzer or overlooker why by an inscrutable combination of train'd wisdom and natural intuition most fully accepts in perfect faith the moral unity and sanity of the creative scheme, in history, science, and all life and time, present and future, is both the truest cosmical devotee or religioso, and the profoundest philosopher.

The third excerpt is from Whitman's long footnote to line 1723 of "Democratic Vistas."

9. "Song of the Universal," 57–61.
10. These lines, from Sophocles' *Oedipus Tyrannas* (471–72), may be translated:

> As sleuth hounds do,
> The Fates pursue.

11. "Universal ownership of property, general homesteads, general comfort—a vast, intertwining reticulation of wealth." (S)
    "Democratic Vistas," 666–67.
12. "Democratic Vistas," 937–47. (S)
13. Ibid., 952–66.
14. "Notes Left Over: Freedom," 16–26.
15. "Democratic Vistas," 368–410.
16. *Specimen Days,* "Carlyle from American Points of View," 75–88.
17. "Democratic Vistas," 540–67.
18. Ibid., 528–35.
19. "Democratic Vistas," 656–64.
20. Ibid., 715–34.
21. Ibid., 756–62.
22. "Poetry To-Day in America—Shakspere—The Future," 299–305. Smuts has inverted the two parts of the quotation.
23. "A Backward Glance O'er Travel'd Roads," 245–46.
24. "Democratic Vistas," 1425–31; 42–50.
25. Ibid., 1375–1403.
26. "Poetry To-Day in America—Shakspere—The Future," 249–59.
27. "Who Learns My Lesson Complete," 1–6.
28. "Democratic Vistas," 806–20.
29. "A Backward Glance O'er Travel'd Roads," 355–60.
30. Ibid., 266–68.
31. "Democratic Vistas," 806–20.
32. Ibid., 1008–17.
33. Ibid., 963–77.

34. Ibid., 988–91.
35. Ibid., 1858–67.
36. Ibid., 1672–86.
37. Ibid., 1965–72.
38. "A Backward Glance O'er Travel'd Roads," 105–12.
39. "Eidólons," 69–72.
40. "Notes Left Over: Ventures, On an Old Theme," 23–27.
41. "Preface, 1855, to first issue of *Leaves of Grass*," 133–49.
42. Ibid., 174–86.
43. "To Him That Was Crucified," 5–13.
44. "Democratic Vistas," 1904–16.
45. "Passage to India," 104–15.
46. "Notes Left Over: Emerson's Books, (The Shadows of Them.)," 47–51.
47. "Passage to India," 10–29.
48. Ibid., 81–87.
49. Ibid., 93–98.

Chapter 7

1. "As at Thy Portals Also Death."
2. "The Dismantled Ship." In his footnote to page 37 of *November Boughs* Whitman wrote of "The Dismantled Ship" and "An Evening Lull": "The two songs on this page are eked out during an afternoon, June, 1888, in my seventieth year, at a critical spell of illness. Of course no reader and probably no human being at any time will ever have such phases of emotional and solemn action as these involve to me. I feel in them an end and close of all."
3. *Specimen Days*, "An Interregnum Paragraph," 7–8.
4. Ibid., "An Early Summer Reveille," 1–14.
5. Ibid., "Cedar-Plums Like—Names," footnote to line 61.
6. Ibid., "Hours for the Soul," 34–42.
7. Ibid., "The Sky—Days and Nights—Happiness," 29–32.
8. Ibid., "Scenes on Ferry and River—Last Winter's Nights," 68–73. Smuts provides the following footnote: "As a most instructive indication of Whitman's evolution, compare this masterly passage with the tone and spirit of an equally masterly passage on the night which appeared in the original edition of *Leaves of Grass* ("Song of Myself," pp. 45–6):
I am he that walks with the tender and growing night,
I call to the earth and sea half-held by the night.

Press close bare-bosom'd night—press close magnetic nourishing
    night!
Night of south winds—night of the large few stars!
Still nodding night—mad naked summer night.

Smile O voluptuous cool-breath'd earth!
Earth of the slumbering and liquid trees!
Earth of departed sunset—earth of the mountains misty-topt!
Earth of the vitreous pour of the full moon just tinged with blue!
Earth of shine and dark mottling the tide of the river!
Earth of the limpid gray of clouds brighter and clearer for my
    sake!
Far-swooping elbow'd earth—rich apple-blossom'd earth!
Smile, for your lover comes.

9. These lines are the aphorism "Language," from Schiller's *Xenia* (1796), written at the suggestion of Goethe. They may be translated as:

Why can the living spirit never be seen by the spirit?
As soon as the soul begins to speak, alas, then can the
    soul speak no more!

10. "Democratic Vistas," 1096–118.
11. "Notes (such as they are) founded on Elias Hicks," 432–41; 448–54.
12. "Preface, 1876, to the two-volume Centennial Edition of L. of G. and 'Two Rivulets'," 104–23.
13. "Passage to India," 194–203.
14. "George Fox (And Shakspere)," 127–48.

Index

Jan Christian Smuts (1870–1950), former prime minister of the Union of South Africa, was a major figure in world affairs. Active in the Boer War and leading South Africa to Union and self-government, Smuts, in his political life, imaged his personal philosophy. He viewed evolution as a series of integrations of forces and ideas, of positions and policies. The practical application of this philosophy is evident in Smuts's Union Party and in his working to help establish the League of Nations. His study of Whitman, written in 1894–95 and hitherto unpublished, anticipates the mature statement of his theory of *Eenheid* in *Holism and Evolution* (1926).

Alan L. McLeod is professor of English and Speech at Rider College, Trenton, New Jersey.

The manuscript was prepared for publication by Barbara Nykoruk. The book was designed by Gary Gore. The typeface for the text is Linotype Baskerville designed by John Baskerville in the 18th century; and the display face is Palatino designed by Hermann Zapf in 1950.

The text is printed on Sebago Text paper and the book is bound in Columbia Mills' Fictionette cloth over boards. Manufactured in the the United States of America.